W9-BVY-116

E P I P H A N Y

**INTERPRETING
THE LESSONS OF
THE CHURCH YEAR**

PHEME PERKINS

**PROCLAMATION 5
SERIES A**

FORTRESS PRESS   MINNEAPOLIS

PROCLAMATION 5
Interpreting the Lessons of the Church Year
Series A, Epiphany

Cover and interior design: Spangler Design Team

Library of Congress Cataloging-in-Publication Data

Proclamation 5 : interpreting the lessons of the church year.
    p.   cm.
    Contents: ser. A. [1] Epiphany / Pheme Perkins. [2] Holy week / Robert H. Smith. [3] Advent/Christmas / Mark Allan Powell. [4] Lent / Cain Hope Felder.
    ISBN 0-8006-4178-7 (ser. A, Epiphany)—ISBN 0-8006-4180-9 (ser. A, Holy week)—ISBN 0-8006-4177-9 (ser. A, Advent/Christmas)—ISBN 0-8006-4179-5 (ser. A, Lent)
    1. Bible—Homiletical use.   2. Bible—Liturgical lessons, English.
BS534.5.P765   1992
251—dc20   92-22973
                                                                            CIP

Manufactured in the U.S.A.   AF 1-4178
96   95   94   93   92   1   2   3   4   5   6   7   8   9   10

CONTENTS

The Epiphany of Our Lord

Lutheran	Roman Catholic	Episcopal	Common Lectionary
Isa. 60:1-6	Isa. 60:1-6	Isa. 60:1-6, 9	Isa. 60:1-6
Eph. 3:2-12	Eph. 3:2-3a, 5-6	Eph. 3:1-12	Eph. 3:1-12
Matt. 2:1-12	Matt. 2:1-12	Matt. 2:1-12	Matt. 2:1-12

Although the Western churches have traditionally emphasized Christmas, the Eastern churches treat Epiphany as the major feast that celebrates the coming of salvation. The Greek word *epiphaneia* means "manifestation" or "appearance." The date of January 6 was calculated on the basis of Luke 3:23 and was celebrated as a feast in the early church, even if it fell on the weekly days of fasting. This feast was felt to be more important than the day of Christ's birth, since it represents the manifestation of Christ as savior to the whole world.

All of the readings for Epiphany refer to the Gentiles coming to see the glory of God. Isaiah's prophecy has been taken up in the New Testament account of the Magi. Ephesians celebrates the new people of God that embraces Jew and Gentile. The story of the Magi has always represented the Gentiles who would come to believe in Jesus as the Messiah. Since the story in Matthew presumes that the new star appears when Jesus is born, some of the early Christian writers wondered how the Magi could have made the journey from Babylon, Persia, or Arabia so quickly. Some thought that they must have had a particularly swift breed of camel.

FIRST LESSON: ISAIAH 60:1-6

The Isaiah reading summons those in Jerusalem to look up and see that the time of salvation has finally come. The other nations will seek the light that shines forth from Jerusalem (vv. 1-3). Israel will look up and see them bringing their wealth to worship God and beautify the city (vv. 4-6). The power of these oracles lies in the fact that they envisage an end to the centuries of exile and oppression suffered by the people. The caravans of foreigners will bring back Jerusalem's children, who have been born far away from their homeland (v. 4). With her city and temple partially destroyed and only some of those exiled to Babylon returned, Israel did not look like a nation poised on the verge of a glorious future.

The prophet's vision reverses all the negative conditions of exile. Where Jerusalem had appeared to be in darkness, now she would shine with God's glory while the surrounding nations sit in darkness (v. 2). Where the people had been carried away from their land and scattered among the nations of the world, the nations would come streaming to Zion and bring with them her sons and daughters (v. 4). Where Jerusalem had been despoiled by foreign conquerors, the nations would bring their wealth to her (vv. 5-6).

The light that shines in the restored city is not merely the splendor of material prosperity that has returned to a war-torn land. It is the glory of God's presence. This theme (vv. 1-3) recalls old traditions of God's appearance, or theophany (e.g., Judg. 5:4-5; Ps. 18:8-16). In these traditions, lightning and thunder, darkness, and earthquakes are all evidence that the Lord, the divine warrior, goes forth to shape the destiny of nations. Isaiah strips the elements of war away from this tradition of God's appearance. All that remains is the light that symbolizes the presence of salvation.

Although some scholars think that these oracles were spoken as the exiles were returning from Babylon to legitimize the new order under the Persian rulers (cf. Ezra 7:15-23), others point out that the prophet does not link God's salvation to any changes in political affairs. These oracles may represent a later situation. When the return of the exiles did not bring the glorious time of peace that had been anticipated, the prophet sought a new vision of salvation. No armies or political arrangements would be involved. God's presence alone would renew the holy city. The wealth that the nations bring is not reparation for what Israel had suffered. It is their testimony to the glory and greatness of God.

SECOND LESSON: EPHESIANS 3:2-12

Written in Paul's name by a follower of the apostle, Ephesians recalls the apostle's life and teaching for Christians in Asia Minor. The author developed this section from themes found in Col. 1:23-28: introduction to Paul, the suffering apostle (Col. 1:23c-24; vv. 1, 13); the apostolic office (Col. 1:25; v. 2); revelation of the hidden mystery (Col. 1:26; v. 6); and proclamation of the content of the mystery (Col. 1:28; vv. 8-9). In Greek, two long sentences make up the passage: (1) vv. 2-7: Paul's apostleship brings the Gentiles into the people of God; (2) vv. 8-12: the mystery of God's plan for the cosmos has now been revealed.

The passage uses the revelation schema as its literary form. This pattern announces that what had previously been hidden has now been made known. This literary form is particularly appropriate to the feast of Epiphany, which celebrates the manifestation of salvation. Paul's mission to the Gentiles is depicted as the unveiling of that divine mystery. He has insight into God's plan (vv. 3-4, 8-9). By preaching Christ among the Gentiles, Paul has also made that plan an effective reality for the readers of Ephesians. Without the apostolic ministry, they would not share in the riches of God's salvation (vv. 6, 8).

The mystery that Paul received through a revelation from God (v. 3) was that the Gentiles would share in the same promises of salvation that God had made to Israel. Paul refers in Gal. 1:12-16 to his vision of the risen Lord as God's call to preach Christ among the Gentiles. He always associated that experience with his violent opposition to the emerging Christian movement (Gal. 1:13; 1 Cor. 15:9). Ephesians retains Paul's description of himself as "least of the apostles" (1 Cor. 15:9) by referring to him as "very least of all the saints" (v. 8) when God gave him the mission of preaching to the Gentiles. However, the readers know that this apostle, who has meant so much to their faith, is imprisoned and soon to be martyred for his bold testimony to the gospel (vv. 1, 12-13). Paul's life before he became an apostle and his struggles to convince the Jewish Christian leaders at Jerusalem that Gentiles could receive salvation in Christ without becoming Jews are no longer an issue.

It may seem strange to read a passage that focuses upon Paul's apostolic ministry when celebrating the feast of Epiphany. Paul is the one to whom the mystery has been made manifest. The truth that Paul knows becomes evident in the world through the community that Paul's preaching has called into being. This community is the body of Christ (v. 6; 1:22-23). The basis for this new community is to be found in Christ's self-offering on the cross, which abolished the division between Jew and non-Jew. Ephesians 2:11-22 has described this vision of salvation as peace and reconciliation in which the formerly hostile parties have the same access to God in the Spirit. Verses 3-4 remind the reader of that account.

The revelation schema, a hidden mystery made manifest, explains why this unity was not recognized before the coming of Christ (v. 5). The apostle's ministry remains unfinished. It is still necessary to summon people to see that this "new human being" (= the "new Adam"), which has been brought into being by Christ (2:15-16), represents the plan of the Creator for humanity (vv. 9, 11). Yet the audience can identify Paul's wisdom and insight in their own experience, since they have become heirs to God's salvation in Christ. This passage can be seen as an indirect appeal to the readers to remain firmly attached to the unity and catholicity of the church. It also reminds its Gentile readers of their own, special place in God's plan.

The universality of this vision even goes beyond the divisions that had separated humans from each other and from God. It has cosmic dimensions as well. Verse 10 affirms that through the church this divine plan has been made manifest to "the rulers and authorities in the heavenly places." Jewish and Christian apocalyptic saw the present age as one in which demonic and other hostile powers turned individuals and nations away from God. Some of these powers are associated with the stars and planetary forces. Jewish and Christian writers thought that the pagan religions of the Gentiles were a form of subjection to such demonic powers (cf. 1 Cor. 10:14-22; Gal. 4:8-9). Now that Gentiles are incorporated into the body of Christ, the hostile powers in the cosmos can see that their domination is at an end.

Christians today may find the language of this vision of God's plan somewhat strange. We are used to the deep-seated religious and social divisions that continue to exist in the human community. We might be much less bold than the apostle (v. 12) in claiming that God's plan for humanity as revealed in Christ is peace, reconciliation, and unity in one community. We may even become incredulous at the claim that such community is the way to disarm the hostile powers that are destroying our world.

GOSPEL: MATTHEW 2:1-12

The story of the Magi led by a star to worship the newborn Jesus is the basis for the feast of the Epiphany. The passage combines two story lines: (1) the recognition of the royal child born in obscurity; (2)

7

the plot to destroy the royal child by an evil ruler. The two have been combined by using the quest for the child as the occasion that awakened the ruler's suspicion (vv. 2-3). Early Christian writers noted the tension between the two plots. Since the star could have led the Magi to the child, they reasoned that the encounter with Herod was necessary so that the Gentiles could learn the testimony to Christ that lay in the prophecies possessed by the Jewish people. Or, they argued, the star was not visible where Herod was.

As told in Matthew, the Magi are not present when Herod learns of the prophecies from the high priests and scribes. He summons them secretly and sends them to Bethlehem with the claim that he too seeks to worship the child as they do. Both the secret summons and the fear that the reader knows has been stirred up in Herod's heart indicate that Herod's intentions are malicious (vv. 7-8). Most modern interpreters resolve the tension between the two story lines by suggesting that Matthew has combined the story of the recognition of the royal child with the more extensive narrative about Herod as the evil ruler who seeks the child's life. The rest of Matthew 2 shows Herod as the pharaoh of the Exodus story. Threatened by the royal child who will be the liberator of Israel, he slaughters the infants. Jesus is taken down into Egypt to be called forth again as God had once called Israel from Egypt.

Both ancient and modern interpreters have noted the contrast between Herod as an illegitimate, earthly king and Jesus as the true king of Israel. Herod ruled the Jewish people by mere power. He was not a legitimate king of Israel. Herod could not make any claim to the Davidic descent that was seen as the basis for messianic kingship in the prophecy to which his own advisers refer (vv. 5-6). Matthew's reader knows, of course, that Jesus does belong to the house of David (Matt. 1:2-17). The Magi show by their obedient departure that they recognize the spiritual nature of Christ's kingship. Indeed, some ancient writers concluded that having left the court of the evil king and found the true king, the Magi could hardly return to Herod. One ancient legend held that the Magi continued to worship Christ after their return home. Then, when the apostle Thomas went to evangelize the East, they were baptized and assisted in his mission.

Translating the Greek term *magos* into English is difficult because scholars do not agree on which meaning Matthew intends. Originally "magi" were the priestly caste of the Persian Zoroastrian religion. But by New Testament times the term could designate a wise person, usually from somewhere in the East; an astrologer, magician, soothsayer, or dream interpreter; or someone who was simply a religious fraud. While it seems clear that the Magi as presented in Matthew are not in the religious fraud or in the negative magician/soothsayer categories, it is not easy to tell which of the other views is intended. The fact that they note the star "at its rising" (v. 2; the older translations "in the East" have failed to render the technical meaning of the expression) does not require elaborate astrological knowledge.

Although some modern readers persist in looking for supernovae, comets (Halley's appeared in 12/11 B.C.E.), or astrological conjunctions of Jupiter and Saturn to explain the star in the story, these attempts ✓ are quite beside the point. As the ancients recognized, the star is not one of the created celestial bodies but a special sign from God. It functions like the pillar of cloud that guided the Israelites in the wilderness. Its most likely origin lies in an Old Testament prophecy, the oracle of Balaam (Num. 24:17), which was understood to refer to the anointed priest or king that God would raise up for the people in the last days. Although Matthew does not allude to Balaam directly, some Jewish traditions place him in the East and even refer to him as *magos*. The star, therefore, is part of the symbolic texture of the story, ✓ which reminds the reader of earlier stories of salvation. It has nothing to do with astronomical observations or with dating the birth of Jesus to coincide with some ancient record of an astronomical event. Indeed, it is not clear that even the reference to Herod should be used to date the birth of Jesus. The Herod of this story died shortly before Passover in 4 B.C.E. Herod, who had killed three of his own sons when he suspected them of plotting to unseat him, is the archetypal evil king.

Another prophecy lies in the background of the Magi story as well: Isa. 60:6. The Magi worship Jesus and offer as gifts the wealth that Isaiah predicted the nations would bring to Jerusalem (v. 11). In the context of the Isaiah oracle, the star signals that Jesus is the light of salvation. By combining this story with the Herod episode, Matthew adds an ominous note. Although this attempt against Jesus' life fails, another ruler, and other high priests and scribes, will take the life of the "king of the Jews" at Jerusalem.

The Baptism of Our Lord
First Sunday after the Epiphany

Lutheran	Roman Catholic	Episcopal	Common Lectionary
Isa. 42:1-7	Isa. 42:1-4, 6-7	Isa. 42:1-9	Isa. 42:1-9
Acts 10:34-38	Acts 10:34-38	Acts 10:34-38	Acts 10:34-43
Matt. 3:13-17	Matt. 3:13-17	Matt. 3:13-17	Matt. 3:13-17

Early Christian tradition associated the baptism of Jesus with Epiphany, since the baptism is the public manifestation of the Lord before Israel. For many early Christian writers God's voice and the coming of the Holy Spirit make this feast a celebration of the mystery of the Trinity. The descent of the divine Son into the waters of baptism was seen as an image of Jesus' incarnation. As such, the baptism of Jesus is evidence of God's compassion for humanity.

The tradition calls attention to the relationship between Jesus and God as depicted in the baptismal story. As God's beloved Son (Matt. 3:17), Jesus will bring that salvation anticipated in the Baptist's call to repentance (Acts 10:37). The coming of the Spirit serves as a sign that redemption is at hand. Jesus' ministry manifests the power of God's Spirit (Acts 10:38). Jesus is not merely another human being with a cause.

FIRST LESSON: ISAIAH 42:1-9

This passage contains the first of the Servant Songs in which the prophet speaks of the calling and mission of a mysterious figure designated as God's chosen. Early Christians saw these prophecies as descriptions of Jesus' own ministry (Acts 8:32-35; Mark 10:45). Many scholars think that Jesus identified himself with the suffering servant of these Isaiah poems. Paul uses the servant imagery to describe his own ministry of bringing the light of salvation to the Gentiles (2 Cor. 5:18—6:2; Acts 13:46-47).

Formally, this passage has three sections: (1) the introduction of Yahweh's servant (vv. 1-4); (2) an oracle describing Yahweh's greatness and the role of a mysterious figure in bringing the light of salvation to the nations (vv. 5-8); (3) an independent oracle about "the former things" and "new things" (v. 9). One of the puzzles in interpreting the servant songs is the mysterious figure called "my servant" (v. 1a). The servant is addressed as Israel (Isa. 49:7) but has exercised a ministry to Israel (Isa. 49:5). The servant could be understood as a righteous remnant within the nation (Isa. 65:13-15) or as a martyr in the persecuted community (Zech. 12:10). In relationship to Israel, the servant's activity appears to be that of an individual whose task is described as bringing justice (vv. 1b, 4). In relationship to the nations, the servant appears as a "light," an image for the people as it exists among the nations of the world (v. 6).

The servant is introduced as one chosen and established by God. This divine election is confirmed by the gift of God's Spirit, which will enable the servant to carry out the assigned task (v. 1). Divine election and anointing with the Spirit reminds the reader of the stories of charismatic leaders in Israel's early history. God would designate persons to lead the nation in times of turmoil (Judges 6; 1 Sam. 9:15-17; 1 Samuel 16). Unlike the private experiences of God that characterize the calling of a prophet, the pattern of divine election confirmed by anointing through a prophetic figure implies that the servant has a kingly role.

The servant's kingly role is confirmed by the emphasis placed on bringing justice (Hebrew: *mišpāt*) to the nations (vv. 1c, 3c, 4b). Justice is traditionally the concern of the king. However, this justice is associated with the Gentiles rather than with Israel. In speeches addressed to the nations, justice implies that Yahweh alone is God; the claims made by the gods of other nations are nothing (Isa. 41:1-5, 21-29). We find the associated condemnation of other gods in v. 8. Yahweh is the only God. Divine glory is not shared with others; nor can God's praises be paid to idols. The basis for this monotheistic claim lies in Yahweh's role as the Creator of everything in the cosmos (v. 5). God is not the source of life for Israel alone. All living beings derive their life from the divine Creator.

How does the servant establish justice among the nations? The hints in this passage are somewhat cryptic. The promulgation of justice will not be made with the loud, public cry that typifies enactments of earthly kings (v. 2). Nor will the harsh punishments of the courts be used to crush those who are already weak (v. 3). Sustained by God's power (v. 1), the servant will persist in this task (v. 4). The expansion of the oracle in v. 6-7 focuses on the people rather than the servant alone. A renewal of God's covenant makes Israel the light of the nations. The peculiar expression *bᵉrît ʿam*, "covenant of the people" (v. 6), suggests a universalization of God's covenant. The word *ʿam* is used in v. 5 to refer to human beings in general. Thus, it appears that the new covenant which Yahweh creates with Israel also affects the nations. Since justice in this covenant requires removal of human suffering and bondage (v. 7), the nations too will participate in the salvation that is to come.

SECOND LESSON: ACTS 10:34-43

Peter's speech in Cornelius' house is the first public proclamation of the gospel to the Gentiles in Acts. It contains four sections: (1) an introduction affirming that God can summon persons from any nation (vv. 34-35); (2) a summary statement of the message of peace through Jesus Christ being preached by the apostles (vv. 36-41); (3) summons to repent in light of the fact that Jesus is God's eschatological judge (vv. 42-43); (4) affirmation that the message is based on the prior testimony of the prophets (v. 43a). Grammatically, the kerygmatic section is very awkward and may have been composed by stringing together common kerygmatic formulae.

The introduction invokes an established maxim about the impartiality of God (vv. 34-35; cf. 1 Pet. 1:17; James 2:1). Paul's use of the same theme (Rom. 2:10-11) shows that it was understood in the context of God's sovereignty over all humanity. God judges all persons according to the justice and mercy evident in their deeds. Both Jew and Gentile stand under this judgment. Here, this principle vindicates the possibility of extending the offer of salvation in Christ to the non-Jew. The fact that God judges and rewards all humans impartially does not make preaching the gospel irrelevant, since in the gospel Christ is revealed as the one who sets the standard for that judgment (v. 42).

Luke's formulation of the kerygma (vv. 36-41) serves as a summary of the presentation of Jesus' life, death, and resurrection in the gospel. God, the Lord of all the nations, sent Israel the message of peace in Jesus (v. 36; cf. Luke 2:14; 19:42-44). Jesus' public ministry begins with his baptism (v. 37). Luke's version of the baptism only mentions the fact that Jesus had been baptized. The episode centers upon the descent of the Spirit (Luke 3:21-22). Here, that gift of the Spirit initiates the deeds of healing that Jesus performs during his ministry (v. 38). This formulation also reminds the reader of Isaiah's prophecy that the coming liberator of humanity would be filled with God's Spirit (Isa. 61:1, cited in Luke 4:18; cf. Isa. 42:1).

Luke describes the miracles as "doing good." The Greek expression for "doing good," *euergetōn*, would have reminded a non-Jewish audience of an important ethical concept in their culture, that of the virtuous person as benefactor. Those who had power, social and political status, or wealth were expected to act as benefactors of their local communities. The emperor was benefactor of the whole empire. Services might include direct material assistance or financing of public projects, or they might involve using one's personal influence with others to gain some benefit. Although Jesus is not a king, government official, or wealthy person, the Spirit makes him the benefactor of an oppressed humanity through the power of healing.

In the gospel, Jesus contrasts his example of sacrificial service with the political or royal benefactors (cf. Luke 22:25-27). Although they may assist others, their aid comes at a price: the benefactors are permitted to dominate the rest of the community. Jesus sets a contrary example. The culmination of his sacrificial service comes on the cross. However, believers know that the cross was not the victory of Jesus' enemies, since God raised him from the dead and showed him alive to those chosen to testify about Jesus (vv. 39-41).

GOSPEL: MATTHEW 3:13-17

Matthew's account of the baptism of Jesus is based on Mark 1:9-11. Like all of the gospel versions, the episode culminates with a divine voice from heaven identifying Jesus as Son of God. Matthew has made some changes in Mark's wording that clarify the public significance of the event. Mark treats the baptism as the call of a prophetic figure— that is, the key revelation is given to Jesus alone. Matthew drops the "he [= Jesus] saw" from the reference to the open heaven (v. 16; cf. Mark 1:10) and changes the "you are my Son, the Beloved" to "this is my Son, the Beloved" (v. 17; cf. Mark 1:11). These changes make the divine announcement a public event.

The wording of v. 17 combines Ps. 2:7 (LXX) and Isa. 42:1 (LXX). We have seen that the servant of Isa. 42:1 has a royal task. Psalm 2

13

describes the king as God's son. Consequently, the combination presents Jesus as God's elect ruler. Matthew has already shown the reader that Jesus has been Son of God from the time of his conception through the Spirit (Matt. 1:18-25). Matthew 2 presented Jesus' claim to be the true king of Israel. Since Jesus has been Son from the time he was conceived, the divine proclamation must intend a relationship between Jesus and God that goes beyond the mere adoption of Israel's ruler as God's chosen (as in 2 Sam. 7:14). The authority of Jesus' teaching in Matthew rests on his unique status.

In addition to revising Mark's narrative, Matthew adds an exchange between Jesus and the Baptist (vv. 14-15). This incident expresses a dilemma inherent in the account of Jesus' baptism: how could God's anointed need baptism? John's baptism was an expression of repentance for sin (vv. 6, 11) in anticipation of the coming of divine judgment (v. 12). Jesus' baptism would seem to be inappropriate on both counts. He is the agent of God's coming, as John's objection acknowledges (v. 14). He is also the sinless one who has suffered for our sins (cf. Acts 3:14; John 7:46; 2 Cor. 5:21; Heb. 7:26; 1 Pet. 1:19). The modern tendency to defer all Christology to the exalted Christ and to presume a human Jesus who struggled through life with all the psychological problems of the rest of humanity obscures the urgency of this question about Jesus' baptism.

The tradition contains a number of explanations. We have noted that one approach saw the baptism as a sign of the humanity that the Son of God assumed out of compassion. Justin Martyr (*Dial.* 8.4; 49.1) hypothesized that the Messiah was hidden even from himself until anointed by Elijah. The Baptist is the Elijah who anoints and thus identifies Jesus as Messiah. Some scholars have suggested that the key lies in Jesus' speaking of his death as a baptism (Mark 10:38-39). Seeing his own fate as part of the eschatological trial of the last days, Jesus sought baptism as a sign of God's protection. This explanation might be applicable to the historical Jesus. Matthew omits the saying about Jesus' fate as a baptism from his version of the Markan story, so this suggestion does not reflect the evangelist's view.

Matthew preserves the tradition that John later asked Jesus if he was the one to come (11:2-6). Even from the evangelist's perspective this exchange is not evidence that the Baptist was certain of Jesus' identity from the beginning. Rather, Matthew answers the question about Jesus' baptism for the Christian reader. The Baptist's attempt to

14

prevent Jesus from receiving baptism reflects a liturgical tradition of ✓ questioning those who presented themselves for baptism (also Acts 8:36; 10:47; 11:17). Matthew 28:19 preserves the trinitarian baptismal formula as it was used in Matthew's church. The explanation offered in the exchange between John and Jesus presumes readers familiar with the church's baptismal practice as well as the confession that Jesus is Son of God.

Jesus' response, "it is proper for us in this way to fulfill all righteousness" (v. 15), employs two key Matthean terms, "fulfill" and "righteousness." Matthew emphasizes righteousness as a quality of the human response to God's gift of salvation, even though this obedience to God's will may result in suffering (Matt. 5:6, 10). Jesus' preaching summons the disciples to a higher righteousness than that required by the religious teachers of the time (5:20; 6:1; some translations shift 6:1 from "righteousness" to "piety," although the Greek term remains the same). The expression "fulfill" is used in connection with prophecy as well as the law (e.g., Matt. 5:17). The prophetic texts that stand in the background of the baptismal story (Ps. 2:7; Isa. 42:1) confirm the statement that Jesus' action fulfills the prophets. Matthew's use of "righteousness" for obedient response to God gives the episode an exemplary overtone. Jesus is the perfect expression of God's will (Matt. 5:48).

Since the term "righteousness" could also be translated "justice," "fulfilling all righteousness" brings us back to the task of the servant in Isaiah 42. The servant is God's elect to make justice prevail among the nations. We have seen that this new experience of salvation implies a change in the normal human ordering of justice. Matthew's Gospel concludes with a mission charge to the disciples. They must spread Jesus' teaching among the nations (28:19-20). Thus, the task of the servant is both fulfilled in Jesus and passed on to the community of disciples among whom Jesus remains present until the end of the age.

Second Sunday after the Epiphany

Lutheran	Roman Catholic	Episcopal	Common Lectionary
Isa. 49:1-6	Isa. 49:3, 5-6	Isa. 49:1-7	Isa. 49:1-7
1 Cor. 1:1-9	1 Cor. 1:1-3	1 Cor. 1:1-9	1 Cor. 1:1-9
John 1:29-41	John 1:29-34	John 1:29-41	John 1:29-34

God's plan of salvation continually challenges human preconceptions. The second servant song opens with a complaint that the servant's mission had been in vain. This view is grounded in a false understanding of the mission God intends for the people. They are not to aspire to the imperial greatness of earthly rulers like Cyrus. Ironically, Paul gives thanks for the very wisdom and knowledge that the Corinthians are misusing because they fail to recognize that the gospel overturns human wisdom.

John's Gospel formulates the tradition about Jesus to underline the greatest paradox of all, the incarnation of the preexistent Word of God as a human person, Jesus. This passage draws out the third traditional meaning of the Epiphany, the incarnation of Christ. For the evangelist, Christ is our only way to knowledge of God (e.g., John 1:18). Early Christian writers concluded that appearances of God in the Old Testament were visions of the Word or of angels (cf. John 8:56).

FIRST LESSON: ISAIAH 49:1-6

The Servant Songs challenged the older Israelite beliefs about God's presence in the nation's history. The established view looked to God to raise up powerful warrior kings so that Israel could be exalted among the nations of the world. Although God had used the Persian king Cyrus as an agent to permit the people to return from exile, they did not return to the glories of the Davidic monarchy. Instead, Israel personified in the servant discovers that she remains an unbroken but bruised reed or a dimly smoldering wick. Is this how God will make her a light to the nations?

Formally, this passage has three sections: (1) the servant's divine call and equipment (vv. 1-3); (2) the servant's despair over apparent failure

16

(v. 4); (3) the new mission from Yahweh (vv. 5-6). This passage repeats the themes of the first servant song (42:1-4), the call and the mission to be a light to the Gentiles. The earlier passage left unclear the question of how the servant would establish justice among the nations. This passage makes it evident that the servant's only weapons are the words that he speaks. God does not give the servant the arrows and swords that kings use to rule their people. Consequently, this vision of the servant is closer to the calling of a prophet than it is to the royal vision of the earlier text.

Some scholars think that the person being addressed in the third section is not the servant/Israel of vv. 1-4, but the Persian ruler Darius. His predecessor, Cyrus, had been given the role of liberating God's people by permitting their return from exile (cf. 45:4, 13). That was the "easy" task. Two generations later, Darius must establish a rule that will provide order and stability for all the nations.

Since the address to the servant employs the same image from Jer. 1:5 of one set apart from the mother's womb in both sections (vv. 1b, 5a), we prefer to see vv. 5-6 as Yahweh's response to the complaint in v. 4. The servant confesses disappointment over apparent failure but expresses confidence in the rightness of his cause before God. The insignificant results cannot be attributed to some flaw in the servant's dedication. How could Yahweh, who claims to be glorified in servant Israel (v 3), accept such results?

The lament in v. 4 does not point to personal suffering or humiliation of the speaker but to the apparent ineffectiveness of those weapons that God had supplied. Some scholars have compared this section to the laments of others who served as mediators between God and a sinful people—Moses, Elijah, and Jeremiah. Like these figures, the speaker is able to separate failure on the human plane from God's reward for faithful service.

The response comes as a surprise. The scope of the servant's labor is no longer Israel but the nations. What appeared useless moments before is really only the prologue to the new task. This new vision has a particular purpose. God's salvation is no longer limited to Israel but will stretch to the ends of the earth. This universal perspective was evident at the beginning of the oracle when the speaker summoned the coastlands and those from afar to hear the account of his mission. This new universal salvation will be the basis for Yahweh's glory, not the political standing of the people, Israel.

17

SECOND LESSON: 1 CORINTHIANS 1:1-9

For this and the next six Sundays, the second reading will be taken from the first section (chaps. 1–4) of 1 Corinthians. In these chapters, Paul contrasts human wisdom, much prized by the Corinthians, with the paradox of the cross and the lowliness of the apostle. Apparently, the gifts of the Spirit enjoyed by the Corinthians led them to think of salvation in terms of powerful speech and wisdom that could be measured by human standards.

Formally, this passage comprises two sections of the Pauline letter form: (1) the greeting (vv. 1-3), and (2) the thanksgiving (vv. 4-9). In the greeting, Paul has expanded his self-identification with a reference to the divine basis for his apostleship (v. 1). Later we learn that the Corinthians are at odds with Paul over the style of his ministry (4:1-5; 9:1-23). But since Paul is fulfilling a divine commission, he is not free to shape his conduct to suit their standards. Paul has also expanded the reference to the addressees (v. 2). They are reminded that a Christian life requires holiness and that the individual churches are part of a larger community of believers. Paul will spend much of the letter correcting the ethical conduct of the Corinthians. He reminds them that their community standards should conform to those of Christians in other churches (4:17; 11:16; 14:33).

Just as the greeting refers to the specific situation of the people to whom Paul writes, so the thanksgiving section points to important themes in the letter that follows. The greeting and thanksgiving sections are bound together by constant references to God and the "Lord Jesus Christ." This repetition reminds the reader that the gift of salvation lies at the heart of Christian life. Without that, none of the spiritual gifts in which the Corinthians take such pride would even exist. It would be foolish of them to think that they could continue to possess spiritual gifts if they ignored the basic requirements of holiness that God expects of all persons.

The irony of Paul's thanksgiving section only becomes evident when one has read the rest of 1 Corinthians. The ancient letter format traditionally included a thanksgiving, usually for the health of the recipient (cf. 3 John 2). Paul created a Christian letter form by expanding the conventional letter format to include a thanksgiving for the faith of the addressees. He usually speaks of the traditional Christian virtues of faith, hope, and love (cf. 1 Thess. 1:2-3). Here, we would expect to find these virtues mentioned following the reference to God's grace. Instead, vv. 5-7 mention "every kind" of "speech (*logos*) and knowledge (*gnōsis*)" and "spiritual gift (*charisma*)."

Paul does include speech and knowledge in the list of diverse spiritual gifts that are given to the community in 1 Cor. 12:8. There, "utterance of wisdom" seems to mean spiritual speech or exhortation. The "utterance of knowledge" that the Spirit gives may refer to early Christian prophecy (cf. 1 Cor. 11:3-16). However, this positive use of the terms "wisdom" and "knowledge" appears in a context where Paul must correct a false understanding of spiritual gifts among the Corinthians. They stress speaking in tongues and apparently claim superiority over those Christians not endowed with that ability. As a result, spiritual gifts have become a source of division rather than unity. Paul insists that the Spirit endows the church with a wide diversity of gifts in order to strengthen it.

At the beginning of the letter, Paul castigates the Corinthians for a false understanding of both speech and knowledge. Apparently, they accept the view of their culture that persons who are able to speak persuasively have a greater wisdom and insight than others (or, as we might say, that the best media campaign establishes the truth of the message). Paul rejects that view because the message of Christ crucified cannot be accommodated to human wisdom (1:18-25). Later he treats a case in which the "knowledge," that is, the theoretical understanding possessed by some Christians, has led them to neglect the truth of Christian love. They must put the welfare of fellow Christians above their own preferences (8:1-13).

When Paul reminds the Corinthians that they must remain holy until the coming of Jesus Christ at the judgment, he may be referring to yet another difficulty in the community: some persons deny the resurrection (1 Cor. 15:12). Their emphasis on dramatic spiritual experiences and gifts in the present may be responsible for this failure; some apparently think that they are already perfected because God has given them such gifts (1 Cor. 4:8; the term "become rich" reappears here). Paul reminds them that Christians live in anticipation of a future shared with Christ. Consequently, even though the traditional faith, hope, and love do not appear in this thanksgiving, the corrections that Paul makes in the Corinthians understanding of speech, knowledge, and spiritual gifts show that faith, hope, and love are at stake in this letter.

GOSPEL: JOHN 1:29-41

The Gospel reading presents a Johannine version of the baptism of Jesus. The evangelist has already told the reader that John's role is to testify to the coming of the Word of God into the world (John 1:6-8, 15). In this version, which is based on traditions about Jesus that are similar to those in the other Gospels but apparently had developed independently, there is no baptism scene. Instead, John testifies about Jesus from a distance. The story about the Spirit descending from heaven like a dove and remaining on Jesus refers to a divine sign that was given to John. John responds by bearing witness to those around him that Jesus is Son of God (vv. 32-34). The Fourth Gospel emphasizes the unity and immediacy of the relationship between Jesus and his Father. It explains that Jesus only prays in order to instruct those around him, since he had no need to pray to the Father (cf. John 11:41-42). Consequently, it would make no sense to speak of a revelation made to Jesus.

Formally, the Gospel reading falls into two divisions, each of which has two scenes. In the first, the Baptist bears witness to Jesus (vv. 29-34): (1) by declaring him to be "Lamb of God" and the expected messiah (vv. 29-31); and (2) by describing the divine sign that enabled him to recognize Jesus' true identity (vv. 32-34). In the second, this testimony brings Jesus his first disciples (vv. 35-42). This episode is set on the day after John's testimony about Jesus. A reminder of that testimony leads two of John's disciples to begin following Jesus (vv. 35-39). Then one of the two, Andrew, goes to bring his brother, Peter, to Jesus (vv. 40-42). Discipleship stories in the Fourth Gospel always conclude with a person who has faith testifying to the truth about Jesus.

In John, faith that Jesus is the Son of God and the only revelation of God is the source of eternal life (cf. 5:24). The Baptist is the first of those persons sent by God to bear witness to the truth (5:33-36). By moving from John's testimony to the actions of the first disciples, the evangelist shows that witnessing to the truth about Jesus is essential to faith. Later in the Gospel we meet such unlikely witnesses as a Samaritan woman, who brings her whole town to Jesus (John 4:4-42), and a man born blind, who testifies to the truth about Jesus in spite of hostile interrogation by the religious leaders (9:1-34).

It is easy to be overwhelmed by the ease with which the Gospel piles up affirmations about the special relationship between Jesus and

God. This section alone contains several of the traditional christological titles of Jesus: Lamb of God (vv. 29, 36), Son of God (v. 34; some manuscripts have the title of the suffering servant, Chosen One, here), and Messiah (v. 41). John's testimony also points to two of the traditional expressions of salvation: forgiveness of sins and the gifts of the Spirit. In the term "Lamb of God," Jesus' death is understood to be an atonement for the sin of the world. In John's account the dove/Spirit remains with Jesus. "Remaining with Jesus" becomes a special theological expression for true belief in the Fourth Gospel. Because the Spirit remains with Jesus, Jesus becomes the source of that Spirit for those who believe. John 7:39 links the outpouring of the Spirit with Jesus' death and exaltation. The power to forgive sin and the coming of the Spirit are given to the assembled disciples by the risen Jesus (20:22-23).

This presentation of Jesus' divine identity and mission should not obscure the equally consistent emphasis upon discipleship as testimony to the truth. The evangelist has not forgotten that the truth about Jesus is known to us only because it has been mediated by human witnesses. Characters like the Samaritan woman and the man born blind show that the chain of witnesses is not limited to the disciples closest to Jesus. The evangelist refers directly to all those Christians whose faith is based upon the testimony of others (John 17:20-21; 20:29).

As this passage indicates, the process of testimony is dynamic. The initial word about Jesus awakens curiosity in the hearers. They have to go find out for themselves who Jesus is. A personal encounter with Jesus transforms the interested hearer into a disciple. For the first group, the question "where are you staying?" (a variant of Matt. 8:18-22; Luke 9:57-60) will lead them to "remain with" Jesus. "Remain" implies that they have become true disciples. In Peter's case, the change is indicated by the name that Jesus confers (v. 42). This dynamic process makes it clear that faith cannot be created through technique, advertising, TV, evangelism, and the like. As Paul reminded the Corinthians, faith depends upon the activity of God (cf. John 10:25-30).

Third Sunday after the Epiphany

Lutheran	Roman Catholic	Episcopal	Common Lectionary
Isa. 9:1b-4	Is. 8:23b—9:3	Amos 3:1-8	Isa. 9:1-4
1 Cor. 1:10-17	1 Cor. 1:10-13, 17	1 Cor. 1:10-17	1 Cor. 1:10-17
Matt. 4:12-23	Matt. 4:12-23	Matt. 4:12-23	Matt. 4:12-23

Isaiah's prophecy that light would come to those in darkness (Isa. 9:2) has echoed throughout the readings of the Epiphany season. Matthew uses it to herald the beginning of Jesus' public ministry (Matt. 4:14-15). The Isaiah oracle goes on to promise a time of peace when all the weapons of human conflict will be destroyed (Isa. 9:5-6). Yet the reading from 1 Corinthians indicates that there was verbal strife and quarreling within the earliest church (1 Cor. 1:10-12). How can Christians proclaim Jesus as Prince of Peace when they cannot even heal the divisions within their own communities?

One clue lies in a fundamental characteristic of all biblical narratives about salvation: They celebrate the success of the least likely. Paul consistently puts the paradox of the cross in the center of Christian life. No human wisdom would see the savior of humanity in someone crucified like the lowest criminal. Isaiah picks two obscure and devastated areas of Israel to receive the light. Jerome reports that Jewish Christians felt it appropriate that the new light should dawn here rather than in the royal capital Jerusalem, since these regions had been the first to feel the yoke of foreign oppression.

FIRST LESSON: ISAIAH 9:1B-4 [8:23B—9:3]

This glowing prophecy of hope follows a grim description of suffering and oppression. The terrible destruction of war leads the hungry people to curse both their political leaders and their God (Isa. 8:21-22). Whether they look to the heavens or to the earth, all they find is darkness. We tend to spiritualize and individualize such passages. The darkness is taken as a sign of the individual lost in sin and confusion until he or she finds the saving presence of God. Certainly, such text can describe the individual spiritual life. But biblical faith speaks to the community about its real existence in the world. Isaiah urges Israel to entrust her national well-being to God rather than to the shifting power blocs in the ancient Near East.

Because Israel's leaders refused to base her national life on the ancient Yahwistic faith, the Lord will permit the invading armies from Assyria to devastate the land (e.g., Isa. 7:1-20). The hungry and discouraged people pour out their frustration against both their leaders and God. They do not acknowledge that this suffering is a just punishment for a nation that has perverted justice (Isa. 1:15-17). Yet, darkness is not God's final word to the people. God can again bring redemption to them.

Formally, this section appears to be a hymn of praise. It is framed by the announcement that those in darkness have seen a great light (v. 2 [1]) and the establishment of a true Davidic ruler, one whose rule embodies God's justice and righteousness (v. 6 [7]). After praising God for bringing the nation joy (v. 2 [3]), three clauses, each beginning with *kî* ("for"), explain how God has brought rejoicing. God has (1) broken the oppressor's power (v. 3 [4]); (2) used the armor of war as booty burned in sacrifice (v. 4 [5]); (3) raised up a ruler able to govern in God's name (v. 5 [6]). These three clauses also reflect the sequence of events that would be required to reestablish the nation after it had been conquered: the oppressor must be destroyed; booty gained must be dedicated to the Lord, not used by the victor; a new Davidic king must ascend to the throne.

Do these hopes stem merely from the political observation that even great empires are overthrown? Or does Isaiah have a new order of things in mind? In order to throw out the Assyrian conquerors, God will have to repeat the miraculous victory against the Midianites. The story in the Old Testament speaks of a small force, one that God required the Israelites to make even smaller (Judges 7), defeating a vastly superior force in a surprise night attack. This episode does not lack human collaboration with God's purposes. However, such an insignificant force could never have won without God's assistance.

Some scholars read these verses as a skeptical response to the opening promise of salvation. In order to establish the nation in peace, God will have to bring about a highly unlikely victory, one that contradicts ✓ all military experience. In order to ensure that peace, every possible implement of war must be dedicated to God by burning. This will include the uniforms that those in the army wear, right down to the combat boots (v. 4 [5]). Such a dramatic change in human affairs will not come about by a simple reshuffling of the power politics of the ancient near east.

Our contemporary experience of politics and war in the Middle East shows that the prophet's words have not lost their ability to illuminate what the struggle for peace really requires. We know that a new order of things is the only solution. Yet, human political wisdom is not able to produce the peace to which humans aspire. The New Testament authors insist that this prophecy never could be fulfilled by another king or superpower dominating the region. It really speaks of a different kind of order altogether, salvation from the sinful human conditions that break the unity with God that is required to have peace. Even Jesus would have to contend with persons who thought that somehow his preaching would bring an end to Roman oppression. The end was not the political victory some hoped for, but centuries later the conversion of the Roman empire by the new faith.

SECOND LESSON: 1 CORINTHIANS 1:10-17

This section introduces the body of the letter, that is, the section in which the business of the letter is discussed. The longer Pauline letters often deal with several themes. Halfway through 1 Corinthians, we learn that Paul has received a letter containing questions (7:1). The opening chapters refer to information that Paul has received from others about the situation in Corinth (1:11). The source of Paul's information, persons attached to the household of a prominent woman in the community, Chloe, need not have come to Paul with the intention of complaining about the situation. The letter that Paul received from Corinth was delivered by others (16:17-18).

Paul seeks to overcome division and factionalism in the community. The word *schismata* ("divisions") does not mean the same thing as "schism" in later church history. It does not suggest that the different groups have broken off from one another. They continue to celebrate the Lord's Supper together—albeit with divisions along socioeconomic lines that Paul also rejects (1 Cor. 11:17-22). In the commercial world of the Greek city, a world familiar to Paul from his trade as tentmaker, persons were encouraged to "be united in the same mind" (v. 10) when they had formed a partnership for a common goal. The unity required is that all parties contribute their share to the purpose for which the partnership was formed.

Living in a wealthy city, the Corinthians knew very well the requirements of a partnership in the commercial sense. They seem to have quite different standards when it comes to the community of faith. In analyzing this passage, we need to recognize that Paul has used some exaggeration in order to make the Corinthians appear ridiculous. The "each" in v. 12 does not imply that every single person belonged to one of the factions. He speaks more generally later of jealousy and quarrels tearing the community apart (3:3). Here, persons appear to be quarreling over which of the apostles was the most enlightened. We know that Apollos had worked in Corinth after Paul founded the community there (3:4-9). We also learn that Apollos is unwilling or unable to return to Corinth (16:12).

Since Apollos had been converted by Priscilla and Aquila and was an eloquent speaker (Acts 18:24-28), some interpreters think that the real dispute was over whether he or Paul had the more profound insight into the gospel. Paul is in the delicate position of sending his associate Timothy rather than Apollos back to the city to deliver this letter (1 Cor. 4:17; 16:10-11). We do not have evidence that Peter had been to Corinth, although the Corinthians clearly recognize his preeminence among the apostles (9:5; 15:5). Perhaps other Corinthians had adopted "Peter" or "Christ" slogans simply out of frustration with the divisions that existed.

Since Paul shifts from the slogans to baptism, we presume that the initial division may have been stated in terms of who had baptized particular persons. We know that Paul's view of baptism makes it the key to the new life in Christ (Rom. 6:3-7). He only downplays baptism in this passage because of the controversy (vv. 13-16). Instead, Paul shifts the reader's attention to his preaching as the real foundation of faith. Without the message about Christ crucified, no one would be saved (v. 17). Paul's solution is to remind the Corinthians of the essential unity in what they believe and to show them how absurd their divisions are.

GOSPEL: MATTHEW 4:12-23

This passage contains two sections: (1) the beginning of Jesus' public ministry (vv. 12-17); and (2) the calling of the first disciples (vv. 18-22). (Verse 23 belongs to the summary passage, vv. 23-25. Its inclusion in the lectionary picks up the reference to Galilee in v. 12 and to Jesus' preaching in v. 17). By combining Jesus' message that the rule of God is near with the Isaiah prophecy, Matthew indicates that God's new order will be established through preaching (and healing, v. 23), not through a "war to end all wars." Eventually, as Paul reminded the Corinthians, that message will be a message about Jesus as crucified and risen.

Many translations fail to indicate the allusion to Jesus' own death in v. 12. Matthew says that the Baptist was "handed over," the same verb that becomes a technical term for the arrest and execution of Jesus (e.g., Matt. 17:22-23). Jesus' public ministry only begins when John is imprisoned. John's death initiates the final phase of Jesus' ministry (14:13). In both instances, as well as in the infancy narrative (2:22), the threat of violence leads Jesus to withdraw.

The Isaiah quotation helps Matthew explain why Jesus' ministry begins in Galilee rather than in Judea or the region of the Jordan where John had been baptizing. Although Jesus' public ministry is restricted to Israel (cf. 10:5-6; 15:24), the allusion to the nations (that is, Gentiles) in the quotation also anticipates the expansion of the disciples' mission to the Gentiles after Jesus' resurrection (cf. 24:9-14, the end will not come until the gospel has been preached throughout the world; 28:16-20). Matthew also alters Mark by suggesting that Jesus had actually moved from Nazareth to Capernaum (v. 13; 8:5; 11:23; 17:24). Tradition holds that Peter's house was at Capernaum. Archaeologists have uncovered a very early house-church on the site of one such house. For Matthew, this movement situates Jesus in the two territories from the Isaiah prophecy.

The story of the calling of the first disciples is taken over from Mark 1:16-20. The same basic story is repeated: first the brothers Peter and Andrew are called, then Zebedee's sons, James and John. In each case, the brothers immediately leave their trade and family to become disciples (vv. 20, 22). This call story is patterned on the Old Testament story of Elijah calling Elisha (1 Kings 19:19-21). The prophet passes by, sees Elisha plowing, and summons him to become a disciple by throwing the prophetic mantle over him. In this story, the disciples are summoned to become fishers of human beings. The fishing expression has negative overtones in the Old Testament, where it suggests entrapment or deceit (Jer. 16:16; Prov. 4:2). Here the phrase has a positive connotation, since it implies missionary activity that leads to salvation (cf. Matt. 13:47-50).

Jesus' message that the rule of God is near implies an urgency that is also reflected in the response of those called by Jesus. In the Old Testament story, Elijah gave Elisha an opportunity to say farewell to his family before becoming his disciple. Here, those summoned to discipleship begin to follow Jesus immediately. Elsewhere, Jesus rejects the request of a would-be disciple to say farewell to a parent (Matt. 8:21; Luke 9:59). This reaction is a paradigmatic case of how persons should respond to God's call. It is paralleled in kingdom parables that speak of the joyful response to a discovery of the rule of God (Matt. 13:44-46, the hidden treasure and the pearl).

We know from Paul's reference to Peter's wife (1 Cor. 9:5) and the healing of Peter's mother-in-law (Matt. 8:14) that Peter did not completely abandon his family. There is no justification in this passage for the claims of those who recruit individuals into Christian cults and insist that they break off their connections with their families. The point of abandoning trade and father lies in the contrast with the Elijah/ Elisha story. The coming of God's rule changes the stakes. There is no time or place for the conventional forms of parting, winding up one's affairs, and the like. The disciples follow Jesus without even bringing in the nets, securing the boat, or stowing their gear. This urgent dropping of all things is like that recommended for the time of judgment: flee the city without even picking up a coat (cf. Matt. 24:15-18).

When the eschatological urgency of early Christianity waned, this example was converted into a moral lesson about single-minded devotion to the gospel. With the development of ascetic forms of discipleship, the stories became examples of radical renunciation of the possessions and family ties that threatened to keep the ascetic from following Christ into the desert. However, the wandering discipleship that these followers assume is not a matter of individual piety or perfection. The commission to become fishers of human beings implies that its justification lies in the urgent need for the gospel to be preached throughout the world. Otherwise, the prophecy about light coming to the nations will remain unfulfilled.

Fourth Sunday after the Epiphany

Lutheran	Roman Catholic	Episcopal	Common Lectionary
Mic. 6:1-8	Zeph. 2:3; 3:12-13	Mic. 6:1-8	Mic. 6:1-8
1 Cor. 1:26-31	1 Cor. 1:26-31	1 Cor. 1:26-31	1 Cor. 1:18-31
Matt. 5:1-12	Matt. 5:1-12a	Matt. 5:1-12	Matt. 5:1-12

The Epiphany season has emphasized God's appearance to save those in darkness. The new order of peace and justice was God's doing or came through agents whom God raised up to lead the people. This message was a necessary antidote to the crushing despair that followed war and exile. It was also a caution to those who thought that human cleverness and political adroitness could restore the nation. However, left unchallenged this message could lead to passivity and resignation. Concern for justice, well-being, and holiness in society could be displaced onto God alone.

Today's readings pick up the theme of discipleship from last Sunday. They focus our attention on what God requires of humankind. Micah 6:8 reduces the whole Torah to a simple requirement, "to do justice, and to love kindness, and to walk humbly with your God." The Beatitudes also speak of the fundamental virtues of the "poor in Spirit" (Matt. 5:3) who love justice more than anything else (Matt. 5:6). Yet it is part of the puzzle of the human condition that our logic and God's never seem to coincide. This dilemma is nowhere more evident than on the cross (cf. 1 Cor. 1:27-29).

FIRST LESSON: MICAH 6:1-8

Micah was a contemporary of Isaiah of Jerusalem, whose description of a renewed Israel we read last Sunday. The corruption of the nation's leaders, kings, priests, and prophets (cf. 3:1-11) was so complete that the prophet has no hopes for renewal or reform among them. God had created a nation out of those who were leaderless at the exodus. Looking back to that period proves a sad indictment of the ingratitude and perversity of human beings.

Formally, this section is a covenant lawsuit (*rîb*). Calling the mountains of the earth and primeval streams to witness the case, Yahweh files a court suit against the people for their lack of fidelity to the covenant (vv. 1-2). The saving acts of God in Israel's early history, the exodus from Egypt and Israel's entry into the promised land, are evidence that God has been faithful to the people (vv. 3-5). The tone of the passage shifts in vv. 6-8. We hear two speakers, perhaps representing a courtroom inquisition. The first asks what sort of sacrifices should be brought to Yahweh (vv. 6-7). The second responds by noting that God does not require the sacrifices described. God demands justice, mercy, and humble (or wise) conduct (v. 8).

The summons to the mountains and streams to attend to the trial reflects old treaty formulae in which the earth and sky are even more primordial than the gods themselves, who were also listed as witnesses or guarantors of the treaty. In a monotheistic perspective, the elements of the cosmos are the only possible witnesses to the covenant that God had made with the people. Thus the elements can judge whether or not the covenant has been broken.

God's indictment begins ironically. Has God perhaps given the people cause for rejecting the covenant? Which of the deeds that follow could they appeal to in defense of their conduct? God brought the people out of slavery in Egypt. God sent them leaders: Moses, Aaron, and Miriam. Micah may intend to allude to the three forms of leadership in his own day. Moses, the author of the Torah, represents what the king or political leaders should be; Aaron, the priestly leaders; Miriam, the prophetic tradition (cf. Exod. 15:20).

Or did God fail to bring the people out of the wilderness into the promised land? When the Moabite king hired Balaam to curse the invading Israelites so that he would be able to destroy the people, all Balaam could do was utter God's blessings on them (Num. 22:1—24:25). Balaam predicts the downfall of the nations surrounding Israel (24:15-25). The fragmentary reference in Mic. 6:5 ". . . from Shittim to Gilgal" also refers to this period. Israel is encamped near Shittim during the Balaam incident (Num. 25:1). Israel crosses the Jordan into the promised land at Gilgal after setting out from Shittim (Josh. 3:1). During the crossing, the Red Sea miracle is repeated at the Jordan river. This time the waters part while the ark of the covenant stands on dry ground in the middle of the river (Josh. 3:9-17). Then the waters return, cutting off Israel's enemies.

The conclusion to Mic. 6:5, "that you may know the saving acts of the Lord," echoes the purpose assigned the crossing of the Jordan, "By this you shall know that among you is the living God, who without fail will drive out . . . the Canaanites" (Josh. 3:10). The Hebrew word for God's saving deeds, z^edaqoth, belongs to the word group "righteous." These are God's righteous or just actions. In the lawsuit, they are evidence that God is just. The judge in a proceeding would pronounce one party right (cf. Exod. 9:27). Thus, this sentence indicates that God is vindicated in the suit against the people.

The dialogue-like exchange that follows (vv. 6-7) seems to request instruction about suitable sacrifices to please the Lord. Micah exaggerates the number involved, since the point is that God does not require any of these sacrifices. Even the shocking possibility of sacrificing a firstborn son as a sin-offering will not be acceptable (v. 7). The Christian reader cannot help but remember that God will make the offering of the firstborn son for a sinful humanity. It is difficult to tell whether Micah is thinking of the sacrifice of Isaac or of the abominable infant sacrifices that occurred in Israel under Manasseh (2 Kings 21:6). Since none of the other sacrifices are violations of the cult, we are inclined to see this verse as a reference to the Isaac story.

The response rejects all such offerings, since Israel's dependence upon cultic institutions has led her away from the fundamental requirements of the covenant. Justice, mercy, and love are all part of that context. They represent the way in which people are to treat others. The final phrase uses an obscure word that has often been translated "humility." That translation, however, does not convey the intellectual overtones of the term that seem to imply insight, prudence, or wisdom.

SECOND LESSON: 1 CORINTHIANS 1:26-31

The religious wisdom referred to in Mic. 6:8 implied insight into how to practice the justice, mercy, and kindness required by God. It presumes the ability to shape religious life in a way that is pleasing to God. The Corinthians were extremely interested in religious experience as a vehicle for attaining wisdom. But they thought of wisdom in human terms as an insight into religious truths and the ability to speak about them in a compelling way. They held that such wisdom made a person superior to the rest of the community. Paul has to correct this false understanding of the kind of wisdom that comes with Christian faith. He must also attack the false spiritual pride that has taken root in Corinth. A human wisdom that exalts its possessor will always stumble at the message of the cross.

Formally, this passage suggests the diatribe style. The author poses a rhetorical question that anticipates a negative answer (v. 26). Three parallel clauses (vv. 27-28) characterize divine election as the reversal of all human evaluations. Verse 29 then states the purpose of this process: to overthrow all human boasting. The theological principle is applied to the specific experience of salvation in Christ, who is the source of all the covenant virtues for the Christian community (v. 30). The section then concludes with a citation about boasting from Jer. 9:24 (v. 31). The only ground for boasting is what God has done in Christ.

Human standards of boasting must be overturned in order to make salvation from God possible. In recent years, the sociological makeup of the early communities ("not many of you were wise by human standards, not many were powerful, not many were of noble birth" [v. 26]) has been seen as an important clue to the appeal of the gospel message. In a society that is hierarchical and aristocratic, individual talent, hard work, and initiative do not count for as much as they do in our society. The Corinthian pursuit of "wisdom," their admiration for rhetorical skill and powerful manifestations of the Spirit, have been seen as typical of persons who had acquired wealth by trading and personal talent but who were frozen out of social esteem and power because of their origins and lack of status. Some of the tensions in the community, such as those between rich and poor at the Lord's Supper (1 Cor. 11:17-22), stem from the attempt of the wealthy to assert their superiority over the poorer members of the community.

Paul's reversal language intensifies their lack of status. God has chosen the foolish, weak, low, and contemptible, those who are nothing, so that all those who hold worldly status will be shamed by the salvation that has come to such persons. The Corinthians are faced with a choice: they can either boast in what Christ has done for them, or they can continue to boast in an empty, human form of wisdom and status. But if they continue to pursue what counts as wisdom and power by human standards, they will lose the very salvation that has lifted them from their lowliness to become God's elect.

GOSPEL: MATTHEW 5:1-12

The theme of reversal, which Paul used to condemn the false standards at Corinth, appears in the teaching of Jesus as well. The God who brought Israel out of bondage is not a God who supports the powerful or founds empires. Salvation comes to the lowly, the suffering, those who turn to God as their only hope. The Beatitudes (vv. 3-12) that begin the Sermon on the Mount can be understood from two perspectives. As an eschatological blessing the Beatitudes refer to God's salvation that will finally be shown to the lowly, the suffering, and the oppressed. As requirements of discipleship the Beatitudes describe the conduct of those who belong to the rule of God.

Formally, this passage consists of an introduction to the Sermon on the Mount (vv. 1-2), followed by a series of beatitudes (vv. 3-12). Several of these beatitudes appear in second-person form in the Lukan Sermon on the Plain. Matthew 5:11-12 (cf. Luke 6:22-23) shifts from the third person of vv. 3-10 to the second person. The beatitude as a form appears in both Greek and Jewish literature. Most of the Old Testament examples are in the third person. They include a description of the recipient who merits a particular blessing (e.g., Prov. 8:34; Ps. 1:2; 2:11; 40:4; Wis. 3:13-14; Sir. 14:1-2, 20). Apocalyptic literature sees the blessing in a radical transformation at the end of the world. The beatitude is a consolation and encouragement to the persecuted righteous. Beatitudes may be associated with woes against the wicked, as is the case in Luke 6:24-26.

Scholars have observed that the Beatitudes are closely related to the messianic prophecy in Isa. 61:1-2. God's salvation is coming upon those who hear and respond to Jesus' preaching of the rule of God. Only the blessings on the merciful and the peacemakers have no parallels in Isa. 61:1-2. They are the two Beatitudes that call upon the disciples to take an active position with regard to other people: to show them mercy and make peace. The other Beatitudes refer either to what the individual suffers or to inner dispositions.

The beatitudes on the poor (v. 3; Luke 6:20b) and the hungry (v. 6; Luke 6:21a) clearly refer to physical poverty and hunger in Luke. Matthew's version, by contrast, refers to the spiritual character of the blessed. The poor are "poor in spirit," and the hungry "hunger and thirst for righteousness." Some interpreters think that Matthew intends to spiritualize an earlier Jesus tradition that spoke of God's concern for those who were actually poor and suffering. However, Matthew retains the blessing on those who mourn (v. 4; Luke 6:21b) and adds another to this first group on those who are "meek" (v. 5). The echoes of Isa. 61:1-2 also imply that those who are actually poor hear good news about their fate (cf. Isa. 61:1). By Jesus' time the needy, meek poor referred to the righteous who depended upon God. They were often persecuted by the wicked. Consequently, both economic and spiritual characteristics were implied by the expression.

Another term that Matthew uses elsewhere for disciples, "little ones" (e.g., 10:42; 18:10), could be a variant rendering of the Hebrew *ʿanāwîm*, which is most commonly translated by the Greek word for "meek" but could also be rendered by Matthew's "poor in spirit." Consequently, Matthew's readers probably heard these Beatitudes as God's promise that their own lowly position as the suffering righteous would be reversed. The land the meek inherit is no longer the territory of Israel but the earth of God's renewed creation (cf. Ps. 37:11; Isa. 60:21-22). At the same time, the righteous could also look to Jesus' own meekness as an example (Matt. 11:29; 21:5). To be meek is not to be a passive sufferer or ineffective in one's witness to the truth.

The Beatitudes in vv. 10-12 point toward the suffering that the righteous must expect to be their lot in this evil world. Verse 11 presumes that the Christian will be verbally abused by others because he or she is a witness to Jesus. The theme of persecution reappears in descriptions of the disciples' mission (10:17-25; 24:9-10). This situation will not change until the end of the world.

The remaining Beatitudes point toward the spiritual integrity of the disciple and to specific ethical commitments. The promise that the merciful obtain mercy from God (v. 7) is grounded in the covenant. It reappears in the Lord's Prayer petition for forgiveness (Matt. 6:11; also 6:14-15; 7:1-2). Mercy implies forgiving offenses suffered, remitting debts owed, and rendering compassionate judgments. "Purity of heart" (v. 8) appears in Jewish ethical writing as integrity, single-minded devotion to God (cf. Ps. 24:3-4; Jesus is "humble in heart," Matt. 11:29). Its antitype in Matthew's Gospel are the hypocritical persons who make great outward show of piety and bind heavy burdens on others, yet are not truly God's servants.

Making peace (v. 9) is our final example of the active devotion to God implied in the Beatitudes. Throughout the Epiphany season we have been reading prophetic promises of an end to warfare. The sections of the sermon that speak of reconciliation and love of enemies show that the injunction to make peace is not limited to international crises. Christians will have plenty of opportunity to make peace in their own lives and communities.

Fifth Sunday after the Epiphany

Lutheran	Roman Catholic	Episcopal	Common Lectionary
Isa. 58:5-9a	Isa. 58:7-10	Hab. 3:1-6, 17-19	Isa. 58:3-9a
1 Cor. 2:1-5	1 Cor. 2:1-5	1 Cor. 2:1-11	1 Cor. 2:1-11
Matt. 5:13-20	Matt. 5:13-16	Matt. 5:13-20	Matt. 5:13-16

The glory of God is often imagined as a dramatic expression of God's power: the overthrow of the Egyptian army at the Red Sea (cf. Exod. 15:6-8) or the awe-inspiring presence of the Lord on Mount Sinai (cf. Exod. 19:16-20), for example. Other dramatic signs of God's presence are evident in the stories about Jesus: the star that led the Magi; the open heavens and the divine voice at Jesus' baptism; or even the total and immediate response of disciples to Jesus' call.

The prophetic texts that spoke of God's salvation as light coming to those in darkness or as liberation of an oppressed people also suggested that God's appearance would lead to an evident and dramatic change in human affairs. Yet the haunting contemporary ring of the prophets' warnings against thinking that human political strategies would bring peace and security reminds us that the old order seems well entrenched. Where is this new manifestation of salvation? As we move into readings about discipleship during the second half of the Epiphany season, we discover that the revelation of God's presence is not out there in the cosmic or political realm but here among us in the community of faith.

FIRST LESSON: ISAIAH 58:1-12

The Isaiah passage raises questions about the restoration of the community in Jerusalem after the exile. Regular worship with the prescribed days of fasting (cf. Zech. 7:5; 8:19) has been observed for decades, yet the country is in economic and social chaos (cf. Neh. 5:1-14). A new king has ascended the Persian throne. Certainly the dawn of peace and justice under a ruler raised up by God does not appear to be anywhere in sight. Violence tears the holy city itself apart (cf. Isa. 56:9-12; 57:1-10; 59:4). Instead of a glorious, restored city, it remains "ancient ruins"

34

that need to be raised up (Isa. 58:12). The prophet places the responsibility for renewal on the people. They must turn aside from evil if their community is to be restored.

Formally, this section is a salvation-judgment oracle. It begins with the trumpet cry summoning the people to hear God's judgments (58:1). The speaker lodges a charge against the people: they come to the temple frequently and seek oracles of God. They appear to honor the Lord while abandoning justice (v. 2). The people raise a question: "Why has God not acknowledged their fasts (v. 3)? The rest of the passage presents God's dialogue with the people: (1) their day of fasting is one of corruption (vv. 3b-4); (2) a series of questions reject their behavior: God's fast is one that brings liberation and justice (vv. 6-7); (3) the ✔ final section is a series of conditional promises (vv. 8-12).

Several features of this oracle recall themes that are well established in the Isaianic tradition: salvation is the coming of light (vv. 8a, 10b; cf. 42:16; 60:1-3); righteousness and glory surround the people (v. 8b; cf. 52:12b). The most significant echo of other Isaiah material occurs in the acts of mercy that make up the true fast: to free the captive (v. 6, 10a), feed the hungry, give shelter to the homeless, and clothe the naked (v. 7, 10a) all reflect the task of the servant of the Lord (Isa. 42:6-7; 49:9-10) and the anointed savior (61:1-8). Those people in the community who wish to fast as God wishes will take upon themselves the mission of the suffering servant.

Scholars have suggested that this oracle presumes a division within the community. Verse 2 suggests persons who are quite content with their cultic worship and their own practice of justice. They are able to combine oppression and economic exploitation with the day of fasting that is supposed to represent one's repentance and conversion to God. (As a friend remarked the other day, the wonderful thing about our modern economic system is that we can sit in church on Sunday knowing that the interest on our money is piling up.) These persons ask about Yahweh's cultic ordinances but neglect the only ordinance that matters, justice. The question of why God does not respond to their fasts (v. ✓ 3a) may reflect a certain disenchantment among the same group.

The judgment against those whose fast is not accompanied by justice is clearly stated in verse 4b, "Such fasting . . . will not make your voice heard on high." By contrast, those whose fast consists in the deeds of justice and mercy described in vv. 6-9 can be sure that the Lord will respond when they call (v. 9a). As described, all the required actions can be performed by individuals. The prophet seems to have concluded that the community itself will remain divided. The wicked will never be heard by God. The just are assured that God brings them salvation. At the same time, the actions that the prophet says are required relate directly to needs of the time: the nation was in bondage to Persia and oppressed by taxes; loans at high rates led to enslavement of those who could not pay; and other disastrous economic conditions prevailed (Neh. 5:1-17). Providing for those who are suffering means feeding the hungry, freeing the debt-enslaved, clothing the naked, and providing for the homeless. These problems afflict our own society. If we expect our worship to be acceptable to the Lord, we have to ask whether we are willing to engage in the concrete actions necessary to alleviate the causes of suffering here at home. Or might the prophet accuse us of hiding ourselves from our own kin (v. 7b)?

SECOND LESSON: 1 CORINTHIANS 2:1-5

After warning the Corinthians that God does not act through what is exalted in the world, Paul turns to the example of his own ministry among them. The style of Paul's ministry at Corinth continued to be a sore point. In a culture that considered the need to perform tiresome manual labor evidence of slavishness, Paul's insistence on working with his hands rather than accepting or demanding support from those to whom he preached was offensive (cf. 1 Cor. 9:1-23). The situation would become even worse when alleged apostles would come to Corinth bringing letters of recommendation from other churches (2 Cor. 3:1), maligning Paul's weak appearance and oratory (2 Cor. 10:10-12), and claiming superior gifts. The fact that some of the Corinthians would be taken in by these false apostles indicates that Paul's argument here was not entirely successful.

Formally, this passage looks back to themes introduced in 1:17-25, picking up the statement in v. 17 that Paul's ministry was to preach the cross of Christ, "not with eloquent wisdom" (i.e., with polished rhetoric). Rhetorically, it should awaken empathy for the speaker by reminding the audience of their past, positive associations with him (cf. 1 Thess. 1:5; Phil. 1:1; Gal. 4:13). The antithesis, not human wisdom, but God's power, was introduced in the earlier section (1:17, 23-25). The passage can be divided into two sections: (1) vv. 1-2 indicate that the form of Paul's preaching is identical with its content; (2) vv.

3-5, that the life of the apostle is a demonstration of the content of his gospel.

Ancient philosophy was understood to be therapy for sick souls. The best and quickest form of healing was for the student to find and imitate a teacher who embodies his teaching. Although there is an irony in Paul's emphasis on weakness, the principle that the life of the teacher ought to exemplify the message would have been easily accepted by the Corinthians. The unity of the apostle and the message would be destroyed if we assumed that the weakness to which Paul refers is something over which he has no control. It does appear from Paul's remarks that he was afflicted by physical weakness or illness (Gal. 4:13-14; 2 Cor. 4:10; 12:7). But in this passage Paul insists that he has chosen a style of weakness to preach the gospel among the Corinthians.

The Corinthians should approve Paul's choice, since the apostle's weakness means that the Corinthians' faith cannot have come from personal attributes of the apostle. It must have come through the working of God's power (vv. 4-5). Paul does not wish to persuade persons to believe by using rhetorical gimmicks. He does not wish to present himself as wise, admired, or influential. Instead, his life and preaching are a demonstration of the paradox that God's saving power is associated with the crucified messiah. This dispute contains a warning for us today. We are sometimes impressed by the techniques of TV evangelists. In some parts of the country, churches have polled their members to find out what extra services should go along with worship—health club and car repair were mentioned in California! Paul would be horrified. Our responsibility is to preach the gospel and rely on God's Spirit working in the hearer to bring others to the Lord. We are not baiting a trap to lure persons into the church.

GOSPEL: MATTHEW 5:13-20

The Isaiah passage told the audience that their acts of justice would bring God's salvation. Paul insisted that the life and activity of an apostle must cohere with the gospel preached. Matthew follows the description of the true discipleship in the Beatitudes with the injunction to be salt (Matt. 5:13; cf. Mark 9:50; Luke 14:34-35) and light (5:14-16; cf. Mark 4:21; Luke 8:16; 11:33). Isaiah 58:6-12 spoke of acts of justice and mercy that went beyond what many in the community thought were required. Matthew 5:17-20 speaks of a higher righteous-ness or justice that fulfills the law and the prophets.

Formally, this section has been composed out of a number of in-dependent sayings. It now falls into two main units: (1) the sayings about salt and light (vv. 13-16); (2) the section on greater righteousness (vv. 17-20). The first section contains Matthew's reformulation of prov-erbs about salt and light that appear elsewhere in the other gospels. Matthew, continuing the second-person address from vv. 11-12, applies each to the disciple/teacher. Matthew also expands the saying about light with a proverb about a city on a hill (v. 14) and an injunction to the disciples. Their "good works" will be the light of the Isaiah promises that draws others to give glory to God (v. 16). The second section contains one independent saying about the permanent validity of the law (v. 18; cf. Luke 16:17), followed by two judgment sayings pointing to conditions for belonging to the kingdom of heaven.

Just as the Beatitudes recalled the prophecies of Isaiah, so the saying about the lamp contains Matthew's use of that imagery. At the same time, the sayings seem to point to the nature of the persons involved until the injunction in v. 16, "let your light shine . . . ," shifts to "good works." We may be intended to link the demand for good works with the Beatitudes that spoke of activities of the disciple, making peace and showing mercy. Or the good works may look forward to the better righteousness that is to be described in the rest of the Sermon on the Mount. The proverbial saying about salt may also contain an implied warning, since unsavory salt would simply be thrown out and trampled. (Matthew uses imagery of being cast into darkness as es-chatological warning; cf. 18:9; 22:13.) But the primary emphasis is not warning but exhortation to live out the reality of the mission to be salt and light for the world. The city on the hill may represent Jerusalem, which was to have a mission among the nations (cf. Mic. 4:1-3; Isa. 60:1-3). These sayings suggest that discipleship which does not meet these conditions is absurd. Christianity does not consist in private illumination or religious experience. It requires good works that can be seen by others as expressions of the glory of God.

The reference to good works provides a point of transition to the discussion about righteousness that follows in the Sermon on the Mount. Nothing in the sermon, or in Matthew's Gospel up to this point, provides the slightest hint that Jesus' teaching might dissolve the authority of the law (v. 17). That saying is also peculiar in the addition "or the prophets" to the question of the law. While it makes sense to speak of annulling the law, it does not make sense to speak of annulling the prophets. Matthew probably added the phrase to an earlier saying about the law, since Matthew understands the ministry and teaching of Jesus as fulfilling the prophets (cf. 1:22; 2:15, 17, 23; 4:14).

Some scholars think that Matthew has edited a group of sayings that came from a conservative, Jewish Christian community. Verses 17-19 could be read as insisting that the law remains valid within the Christian community (v. 18). Verse 19 is phrased in terms of a legal debate over weighty and light commands in the law. It suggests a position that refused to distinguish among the commands in the law; all are equally binding. By shifting the emphasis from fulfilling the law to fulfilling the Scriptures and prophets, Matthew leads us to think of Christ as the one who brings what the law and the prophets were only aiming at. This interpretation preserves the integrity of the Jewish law without committing the Christian community to continue observing the law.

Verse 20 shifts the issue of observance yet again. The will of God that the law claims to embody is imperfectly lived by its custodians, the scribes and Pharisees. Their practice of the law will continue to be contrasted with the wholehearted integrity of Christian discipleship (cf. Matt. 23:1-28). Their teaching does not gain them entry into the rule of God; worse, it even prevents others from doing so (Matt. 23:13). Verse 20 also provides a bridge to the rest of the Sermon on the Mount. The reader still needs to know what is this greater righteousness that fulfills the true intention of the law and the prophets. Matthew 5:21-48 provides concrete examples of what it means to live out this greater righteousness. Verse 48 comes to an even more astonishing conclusion: "Be perfect . . . as your heavenly Father is perfect."

Sixth Sunday after the Epiphany

Lutheran	Roman Catholic	Episcopal	Common Lectionary
Deut. 30:15-20	Sir. 15:15-20	Sir. 15:11-20	Deut. 30:15-20 or Ecclus. 15:5-20
1 Cor. 2:6-13	1 Cor. 2:6-10	1 Cor. 3:1-9	1 Cor. 3:1-9
Matt. 5:20-37	Matt. 5:17-37	Matt. 5:21-24, 27-30, 33-37	Matt. 5:17-26

Deuteronomy presents a choice: either love God, follow God's justice, and prosper; or turn away from God and perish. The prophets chastised Israel for turning from God. They also formed a vision of the renewal that could come from God after the devastation of war, exile, and foreign domination. Last Sunday we saw that the holiness which would be a light to the nations was to be found in the hearts of individuals who turned to God. In the Sermon on the Mount, Jesus proposes a righteousness that goes beyond the commandments of the law and asks people to change their inner feelings so that the sources of injustice like anger, lust, deceit, and greed do not arise. In that sense, Jesus' teaching brings the law to its completion.

We have also heard the prophets speak of God sending the Spirit to special persons who could renew the people through their leadership. Jesus receives the Spirit in a special way as God's chosen. However, this gift is not limited to the great heroes of faith. Paul insists that no one at all could have faith in Jesus, the crucified, unless God's Spirit were working in that person's heart (1 Cor. 2:9-10).

FIRST LESSON: DEUTERONOMY 30:15-20

This passage presents a summary of the choice that the nation faces. If they live out their covenant with God faithfully, they will prosper in the land that God had promised to their ancestors. If they turn aside from God's commands, the covenant will be broken and God will not permit them to continue in the land. Obedience should not be thought of as a compulsion born of fear, as with a child who only behaves when a parent is around or a reward is in sight. Obedience to the covenant commands is born out of the love for God (v. 20; cf. Deut. 6:5) that results from all the blessings that God has already given the people (Deut. 29:10-15).

Formally, this passage concludes a section of Deuteronomy marked as "words of the covenant" (29:1). It represents the decision to accept or reject the covenant with God: (1) the choice is presented (vv. 15-18); (2) witnesses to the covenant are called (v. 19a); (3) a decision is demanded (vv. 19b-20). The formal patterns in this section may have been used as part of a liturgy of covenant renewal. The author of Deuteronomy conceives the entire book as an example of the covenant choice. It opens with, "See, I have set the land before you; go in and take possession" (1:8). Entering the land is one of the blessings of God for which covenant obedience is the appropriate response. Deuteronomy 30:15-19 echoes the opening words, "See, I have set before you today life and prosperity, death and adversity. . . . Choose life."

The theology of Deuteronomy is sometimes described in terms of the sin-repentance-renewal scheme that results when the people have broken their covenant with the Lord (cf. Deut. 10:12—11:32). However, it is also possible to see the message of Deuteronomy as one of blessing. The covenant itself provides the structure that gives life to the community. Consequently, its well-being in a concrete sense depends upon preserving the relationship with God that has been established in the covenant.

Sometimes people imagine that the covenant was broken because its stipulations were too harsh or difficult. Deuteronomy does not hold that view. Just before this passage, the author assures us that God's commands are not distant or impossible. The law can be kept by human beings (30:11-14). All that are required are worship of God alone, justice and mercy toward the weak, honoring of one's parents, administration of justice within the community, fair play between neighbors, and other details such as rules for the practice of war. All communities require some form of legislation about such matters if they are to survive. In Deuteronomy, God has set Israel in the land and has already blessed her. She cannot plead some overwhelming needs in the political or economic order to justify turning away from the covenant.

We find other examples of the covenant ceremony in Exod. 19:3-9 and Josh. 24:15-24. Entering into the covenant requires that the people commit themselves to the Lord wholeheartedly. Scholars have noted a difference between the other two examples and our passage. In the other examples, the people's affirmative response to the decision placed before them is recorded. Here there is no response by the people. The affirmative response certainly would have been part of a covenant renewal ceremony. By omitting that step in the covenanting process, Deuteronomy places the question of life or death, obedience or disobedience, before the reader. We are drawn into the burden of human responsibility for those choices that represent turning away from God. We are warned that such choices, however good they may seem at the time, come with fatal consequences.

SECOND LESSON: 1 CORINTHIANS 2:6-13

The Corinthians have overvalued human wisdom and rhetorical skill. Paul has insisted that the story of the cross destroys all human claims to wisdom or power. God does not work through the wise and powerful but through the weak. Even the apostle must see to it that his ministry conforms to the pattern established by the cross. Suddenly, Paul seems to shift gears and to promise the Corinthians what they have been demanding, a wisdom for the elite, the enlightened or spiritually mature (v. 6). Although Paul permits his readers to think themselves among "those who are spiritual" rather than those instructed by human wisdom (v. 13) throughout this passage, he cuts them down to size in 1 Cor. 3:1-4. Spiritually mature persons would not engage in the factionalism and jealousy evident at Corinth.

Formally, 1 Cor. 2:6-16 employs what has been described as the revelation schema, wherein a mystery hidden in God's plan from the beginning is made known to the elect. In Jewish apocalyptic, the mystery concerns the working out of God's plan of salvation at the end of the age. Non-Jewish variants in the mystery religions or in philosophical schools referred to the revelation of some ritual actions or higher doctrines only to those persons who had passed through the appropriate degrees of initiation. The Corinthians probably thought that Paul was speaking in the philosophical sense where higher truths are hidden from the immature and known only by an elite. Paul is clearly using the revelation schema in the Jewish apocalyptic sense, however. The issue is the plan of salvation, that is, the cross (vv. 8-9). This passage can be divided into two parts: (1) the wisdom God has prepared for the elect (vv. 6-9); (2) how humans come to know that wisdom through the Spirit (vv. 10-13).

The first section agrees that there is a Christian wisdom that is not to be identified with the wisdom of this age. The proof that the two cannot be identified is taken from the fact of the crucifixion. Had the ruling powers been able to perceive God's plan, they would not have crucified the "Lord of glory" (v. 8). The expression "Lord of glory" transfers one of God's attributes, glory, to Jesus on the cross. Paul also links glory with the believers, since Jesus makes a share in that glory possible for us (v. 7; cf. Rom. 8:18, 21, 30; 2 Cor. 4:17). Scholars disagree over the meaning of the expression "rulers of this age" (vv. 6, 8). Some think it is merely a poetic way of speaking about the political authorities responsible for Jesus' death. Others find in it reference to the demons thought to rule nations and interfere in human affairs. The reference to the rulers as doomed to pass away (v. 6) as well as the apocalyptic meaning of mystery that is presupposed here make it possible to see a reference to more than merely human calculations in this passage (cf. the expression "god of this world" in 2 Cor. 4:4).

The passage cited as Scripture in v. 9 cannot be identified with any specific text (cf. Isa. 64:4; Ps. 31:20). The expression "those who love God" appears in Rom. 8:28. The passage may be a Pauline creation out of similar-sounding phrases. What it does is to shift emphasis from the fact of God's end-time revelation to the recipients, those who love God.

The shift in v. 9 prepares for the treatment of the person who receives insight into the divine mystery in vv. 10-13. This discussion employs a principle widespread in Greek philosophy: like is known by like. In this case, one who is not spiritual cannot understand spiritual things. No one who lacks the Spirit of God can understand what is in God's plan (vv. 10-11). The subtle irony in these verses was probably invisible to the Corinthians until Paul rebuked them directly in 1 Cor. 3:1. All Christians receive the Spirit (cf. 1 Cor. 12:3). The Corinthians pride themselves on spiritual gifts, yet they have shown themselves unable to comprehend the mystery of the cross. But those who do not comprehend the Christian mystery are outsiders; they do not have the Spirit. If the Corinthians persist in their immature behavior and preoccupation with human wisdom, they cannot be among the elect to whom God has revealed the truth of salvation.

GOSPEL: MATTHEW 5:20-37

The superior righteousness that Jesus requires of the disciples (v. 20) is illustrated in a series of examples. Throughout the centuries Christians have wondered how they are to apply the so-called hard sayings of Jesus. Some of these sayings seem to be aimed at a person's inner disposition rather than at actions that might or might not result from such a disposition (anger, vv. 21-26; lust, vv. 27-30). But others recommend concrete forms of action (oaths, vv. 33-37; divorce only in the case of sexual immorality, vv. 31-32). Martin Luther saw the Beatitudes as examples of the gospel: God's promise of salvation. The radical sayings in this section have the form of laws that humans will never achieve. Our attempts only remind us that humans are always sinners before God. We do not have to measure up to such commandments because God has extended salvation to a sinful humanity.

Formally, this section consists of a series of antitheses shaped by Matthew out of earlier tradition. Antithesis is a type of speech developed in the Jewish tradition in which a point of doctrine is cited, then rejected. Each begins with some form of "You have heard. . . ." Earlier teaching is frequently cited from Scripture. Then "But I say . . ." establishes Jesus' teaching as something that either revokes or radicalizes what the tradition had taught previously. The divorce prohibition (vv. 31-32) is the most straightforward example of the form. Each of the others contains some form of expansion in the form of parable, illustration, reference to judgment, or rhetorical question. The first three are presented as legal ordinances. The last three are presented as absolute commands or prohibitions.

Jewish ethical writers warn about anger (vv. 21-26). Although today we tend to accept the psychological directive that people should express their anger, the ancient world expected the virtuous person to overcome anger. Jesus employs irony in this section, since the more trivial manifestations of anger are said to merit trial before a higher court: for anger, a local court proceeding; for insulting another, trial before the Sanhedrin; for calling someone a fool, eternal damnation. This passage seems to mock those who think they could control human behavior by making more and more detailed laws (as, for example, the early New England Puritans did. A special Boston ordinance sought to stamp out the worldly vanity of long hair on males.) It contains additional recommendations that suggest the real point is not whether a person loses his or her temper, but whether an individual is committed to seeking reconciliation. The requirement to be reconciled before bringing a gift to the altar (v. 23-24) recalls the prophets' emphasis on justice and mercy as requirements of acceptable cultic activity.

Jewish ethical writers also condemned looking at a woman so as to excite one's sexual passion for her (e.g., Num. 15:39; Sir. 23:4-6). Jesus' saying (vv. 27-30) radicalizes that position by equating lust with adultery, largely thought to be a crime against the husband's property. It also insists that males are responsible for their sexual passions rather than falling back on the common excuse that women are guilty of causing passions that males cannot be expected to control. The seriousness of this teaching is underlined by the vivid sacrifice that one should be ready to make in order to follow it: an eye or a hand could be cut off; that is, one cannot appeal to natural bodily functions in such a way as to avoid responsibility for one's sexual conduct.

The prohibition of divorce (vv. 31-32) is formulated from the perspective of the male. Jesus follows the stricter interpretation of some Jewish teachers that divorce is not permitted except in cases of sexual immorality, an obscure expression that might refer to prohibited degrees of kinship (cf. 1 Cor. 5:1). The saying is also formulated in terms of the husband's responsibility for what divorce does to the wife. She becomes an adulteress, presumably because she has to marry another in order to survive in a traditional society. Since divorce was readily available to both males and females, this saying was no less countercultural in the first century than it is today.

The question of oaths (vv. 33-37) also appears in James 5:12, which may reflect an earlier form of this tradition. Two arguments are given to reject oath-swearing altogether. One is theological. The Ten Commandments prohibit taking the Lord's name in vain. By Jesus' day the divine name was not pronounced but various circumlocutions had been worked out. They are all rejected. If it is wrong to swear by God's name, then it is also wrong to make some form of substitution. The second argument concerns the integrity of a disciple's word. We only ask people to swear oaths because we do not trust them to speak the truth. A person devoted to God would not need the restraint of an oath upheld by God's holiness.

Seventh Sunday after the Epiphany

Lutheran	Roman Catholic	Episcopal	Common Lectionary
Lev. 19:1-2, 17-18	Lev. 19:1-2, 17-18	Lev. 19:1-2, 9-18	Isa. 49:8-13
1 Cor. 3:10-11, 16-23	1 Cor. 3:16-23	1 Cor. 3:10-11, 16-23	1 Cor. 3:10-11, 16-23
Matt. 5:38-48	Matt. 5:38-48	Matt. 5:38-48	Matt. 5:27-37

Human communities are manifestations of God when they exhibit characteristics that are associated with God. Holiness is one of the most fundamental attributes of God. It suggests separation from everything that is touched with imperfection. In the Old Testament, holiness is associated with purification rites. The ritual cleanses impurity or sin and so enables the individual (particularly the priest) to enter the presence of God. Archaic religious sentiment held that if anything impure approached God, it would be destroyed (cf. Exod. 19:21-23).

This Sunday's readings develop the theme of holiness as it is reflected in the communities of faith. The Leviticus reading introduces a collection of fundamental precepts, many from the Ten Commandments, with the command to be holy as God is holy (19:2). A similar injunction concludes the antithesis section of the Sermon on the Mount (Matt. 5:48). In both cases the community attains its likeness to God through wholehearted obedience to God's command. Paul draws upon a different holiness image, that of the temple as a holy place. The true Christian temple is not a building but the community of believers (1 Cor. 3:16-17).

FIRST LESSON: LEVITICUS 19:1-2, 9-18

The section of Leviticus is often referred to as the holiness code. It is addressed to the whole people as not merely those who serve God in the temple. The author shared the view of the priestly tradition that Israel could be drawn into the presence of God where she would remain secure. The precepts in this section of the book include the major commands of the Decalogue as well as other statutes against mixing cattle and seed of different kinds (v. 19). Prohibitions against mixing

46

disparate things always seem peculiar to outsiders. However, the image of holiness as purification would imply that things of different kinds should not be combined. Disparate mixtures violate the ordered boundaries that God established at creation.

Formally, Leviticus 19 collects a varied group of statutes under the rubric of being holy as God is holy (v. 2). The precepts are in the apodictic form, "you shall (shall not . . .)," rather than the conditional form, "if you do . . . , then x will. . . ." As a whole Leviticus 19 deals with the conduct of individuals in the routines of daily life. The obligation attached to such precepts is intensified by the reminder that the speaker is the Lord (vv. 3, 4, 10, 12).

The commandments in this chapter define what it means for the community of Israel to be holy as God is holy. Although some of the more eccentric commandments refer to customs that are not of concern today (e.g., how males should trim their beards, v. 27; tattooing or cutting the body in mourning, v. 28), the more general commands have hardly gone out of style—for example, those that define the meaning of justice as providing for the poor (vv. 9-10), honesty in dealing with others, especially in business (v. 13), and assistance for the handicapped (v. 14).

Scholars have observed new emphases in the social dimensions of the legislation in this chapter. The mother comes first in the command to honor one's parents (v. 3). Perhaps loosening of the family structure after the exile had left women more vulnerable than they had been when the tribal patriarchy was intact. If something happened to her husband, a woman might not have been able to return to her father or brothers. The command not to strip the fields completely bare at the harvest (vv. 9-10) has a social function in Leviticus. It provides a way for the poor in the community to obtain food. Originally, such practices had no social function. In primitive times, some of the fruits of the harvest were left as offerings to the powers in the earth responsible for the fertility of the land. As we learn from the prophets, such superstitions have no place in Israel. The crops are God's gift. The bounty of the land depends upon justice in the society. Perhaps our food banks, which gather food from churches and collect edible but unsalable food from restaurants and stores to distribute to the poor, are a good modern incarnation of this concern.

Other familiar commandments take on additional definition. The prohibition against theft, which originally referred to outright robbery

(Exod. 20:15), has been expanded to include all underhanded dealings. They are a way of dishonoring God's name (vv. 11-12). Other commands prohibit the stronger from using physical or economic advantages to oppress the weaker members of society (vv. 13-14).

The final group (vv. 15-18) concerns how judgments are given in legal proceedings. All persons should be treated equally. One should not malign others or seek gain through "the blood of your neighbor" (vv. 15-16). The commands to love the neighbor are situated in this context (vv. 17-18). Hate and love are not emotional states here, but expressions of how people deal with one another. Grudges and revenge lawsuits are rejected. The conclusion to this set of precepts is a moral commonplace, "love your neighbor as yourself" (cf. Mark 12:31). Situated in the context of rulings about justice, retaliation, and lawsuits, the maxim has a bite to it. How many of us think of this saying when we are threatening to get back at someone through the power of our legal system?

SECOND LESSON: 1 CORINTHIANS 3:10-11, 16-23

Paul returns to the problems of division within the Corinthian church. Boasting in human wisdom will destroy its relationship to Christ (vv. 18-23). A series of architectural analogies serves to indicate why the situation in Corinth should not be permitted to continue even though the Corinthians themselves were not concerned about the problems that Paul addresses in this section of the letter.

Formally, this section contains an extended analogy based on the process of building and decorating a structure (vv. 11-15); an application to the community that identifies the building as God's temple (vv. 16-17); and a hortatory section that returns to the issues in the argument of 1 Cor. 1:18—2:16 (vv. 18-23). The dialogical style of the diatribe is evident in the use of "Do you not know . . ." (v. 16; cf. 5:6; 6:2; 9:13) and the challenge "If you think . . ." (v. 18; a formula that is repeated at 8:2 and 14:37). Paul bolsters the authority of his concluding argument with two Scripture citations about human wisdom from God's perspective (vv. 19-20) and a common Stoic maxim about the wise person (v. 21).

Paul develops the architectural metaphor by describing his role as that of the architect or master builder who sets the foundation (v. 10). Paul's authority to correct the Corinthians lies in the special divine commission ("grace" in v. 10) that he holds as the founder of that particular community (cf. 4:15-17; 9:1-2; 2 Cor. 3:1-3; 10:12-16). Elsewhere, he suggests that his role as apostle/church founder kept him from going into churches founded by others (cf. Rom. 15:20; 2 Cor. 10:14-15). As with any building, other workers are responsible for much of what goes on the foundation. Paul issues a general warning. Those building on the foundation must take care that what they add suits the structure. Given the earlier arguments in the letter, the reference to Jesus Christ as the foundation must mean that what is built on the foundation must be a suitable expression of the gospel of Jesus crucified (e.g., 1:23; 2:2).

With v. 16, Paul switches from the process of building to the finished work. It is the Corinthian community understood as God's temple (cf. 2 Cor. 6:16; Eph. 2:21). This image of the community was developed out of the Old Testament picture of God dwelling with the people (e.g., Ps. 114:2) and the vision of the Temple in the new age (Ezek. 40–48; Mark 14:58). Some of the Corinthians still frequented the cults of pagan temples in their city (cf. 8:10; 10:14-21). They are aware of the special sanctity of holy places. Defiling temples was a serious crime; it was felt that if the community did not search out and punish the offenders, the gods would do so. By making the community God's holy place, Paul can use that sense of the temple as holy to show the Corinthians that the state of their community is not indifferent. Verse 17 invokes God's judgment against any person whose behavior contributes to destroying the community. Sociologists have observed the erosion of communal values and participation in twentieth-century America. We may be guilty of destroying rather than building on Christ as foundation in our own way through indifference and neglect.

Verses 18-23 return to the contrast between human and divine wisdom. The false views of wisdom among the Corinthians are endangering the community. They can possess "all things" (v. 21) as the philosophers claim to do, if they remain united with Christ and through Christ with God.

GOSPEL: MATTHEW 5:38-48

For Matt. 5:27-37, see the Sixth Sunday after the Epiphany.

The sections on nonretaliation and love of enemies seem to separate the Sermon on the Mount from any realistic social ethic or legal principles. We could certainly build a community around the precepts of

Leviticus. We could even adapt the sermon's first four antitheses as standards of community behavior, as was done in monastic communities. But nonretaliation and love of enemies cannot be generalized to apply to groups of people and to nations, or so we might argue. Martin Luther suggested that the Christian can morally accept the disadvantages that would come from following such commands himself or herself but the same Christian as a public official would be bound to punish evil. Christians would lack love for those who are the victims of aggression if they were unwilling to resist evil or to engage in war on the basis of these principles. In a world where most persons act out ✓of evil motives, we cannot act as though all were Christians.

Formally, Matthew is continuing the antithesis form that began in 5:21. The evangelist has created two antitheses from common tradition (cf. Luke 6:27-36). The first antithesis (vv. 38-42) cites the principle of retributive justice from the Old Testament law (v. 38). The counterthesis is in the form of an apodictic command prohibiting a disciple from seeking to oppose (i.e., through legal action) an evil person (or evil as an entity. The Greek could mean either person or thing; v. 39a). The statement of principle is then followed by a series of illustrations (vv. 39b-42). The second section revises the "love your neighbor" command to make it permit or encourage hatred of the enemy (v. 43). It is followed by a double apodictic command to love the enemy and pray for the persecutor (v. 44). Two arguments, positive (v. 45) and negative (vv. 46-47), for doing so follow. The summary in verse 48 revises a tradition retained in Luke 6:36 to be merciful as God is merciful. Instead, Matthew has "be perfect" as God is perfect. This expression could be a rendering of the principle of Lev. 19:2 to be holy as God is holy. As such it can apply to the whole section of antitheses, not merely those about nonretaliation and love of enemies. It forms an inclusion with the exhortation to a greater righteousness in Matt. 5:20.

Although we often think of "an eye for an eye and a tooth for a tooth" (v. 38; cf. Exod. 21:24; Lev. 24:20b; Deut. 19;21) as unusually harsh, it represents a common legal principle. The point was to establish ✓ limits to penalties so that an injury did not initiate an escalating cycle of violent retaliations. The apodictic command not to seek retaliation of any sort against the evildoer is one that we would hardly entertain today. Perhaps some individuals might forgive those who have injured them rather than take action, but we could not have a community as a whole based on such a principle. Paul's comments about the lawsuits the Corinthians were bringing against each other show that he was familiar with this principle but does not expect the Corinthians to accept it (1 Cor. 6:1-8).

The examples only sharpen the problem. They encompass a number of situations from violence to the encounter with the occupying Roman soldiers to simple requests for money. Each example specifies what it means not to resist evil. The reaction of the disciple is not passive suffering. In each case the disciple will do more than the actions being ✓ requested. If a person strikes you, offer yourself again (v. 39b). If someone would sue you, surrender more than the suit demands (v. 40). Since the law held that the coat could not be taken from a person in pledge even overnight, the tunic/cloak formulation appears to be directed against a provision that was intended to protect persons from losing something necessary to survival. The soldier demands services; go twice as far, that is, beyond the limit that edicts of Roman governors established to protect subjects from abuse (v. 41; cf. Mark 15:21). Do not refuse the beggar or the person who asks for a loan (v. 42).

There is no command to hate the enemy in Judaism. Greek popular morality, however, often spoke of benefiting friends and harming enemies. The evangelist has probably modified the command to love one's neighbor from Lev. 19:18 to create the opening thesis (v. 43). Early Christians consistently recognized their obligation to pray for or respond gently to those who persecuted, reviled, or cursed them (cf. Rom. 12:14; 1 Pet. 3:16). The positive grounding for this command lies in a) the nature of God (v. 45). Similar injunctions can be found in Greco-Roman moralists, although in their case the gods are detached from what humans do. The wise man is also detached from human passions. Love of enemies therefore becomes evidence of a person's moral superiority to them. The negative examples (vv. 46-47) represent ethics by contrast. Anything less than love of enemies cannot be a reflection of God or of the Christian's status as a child of God. To love friends, greet associates, and the like are no indication of a person's character.

By combining apodictic statements with examples and analogies, Matthew shows that Jesus is not another teacher of the law. The response of the disciple is governed by the love that goes beyond what the rules require. Though most of us react with skepticism if asked whether we follow teaching like this, we should recognize that Jesus is not simply proposing an ideal to humble human pride. Nonretaliation and love of enemies are intended as principles for a Christian life. We can add

51

our own examples to those provided in the Gospel. What about lawsuits when we are annoyed or angry with someone but have not suffered any injury? What about our support for stricter mandatory sentencing? What about the rhetoric of enmity and hatred that our political leaders use when they seek to justify military action in another country? We are a long way from meeting the challenges posed by Jesus' sayings.

Eighth Sunday after the Epiphany

Lutheran	Roman Catholic	Episcopal	Common Lectionary
Isa. 49:13-18	Isa. 49:14-15	Isa. 49:8-18	Lev. 19:1-2, 9-18
1 Cor. 4:1-13	1 Cor. 4:1-5	1 Cor. 4:1-5, 8-13	1 Cor. 4:1-5
Matt. 6:24-34	Matt. 6:24-34	Matt. 6:24-34	Matt. 5:38-48

It is difficult to discern God's presence in the world when we see international conflict, social turmoil, rising rates of crime, and fragile economic cycles. Although we often imagine that trust in God's compassion and care must have been easier in a less complex world, this Sunday's readings show that believers have always had to deal with the gap between what appears to be the case and God's perspective. The Israelite exiles suspect that God has forgotten them (Isa. 49:14). They must be reassured that it is impossible for God to forget the chosen people. God will bring them out of the time of distress.

Jesus challenges the pressing anxiety about material security that dominates our lives. We may react by thinking that he never had to worry about keeping up payments on the house, school tuition, or medical and nursing costs for elderly parents. We forget, of course, that over half the children born in this time would die before age two and most adults would die before forty. We forget that taxes to the Romans, tithes to the priests, and field rents would impose on most of Jesus' audience financial burdens as large as our own. Nature herself was capable of sudden and devastating changes. Like Isaiah, Jesus insists that God is not far off and isolated from our lives but is present to help.

FIRST LESSON: ISAIAH 49:13-18

For Lev. 19:1-2, 9-18, see the Seventh Sunday after the Epiphany.

The reading opens with a hymn of praise; yet the real situation of the people is voiced in v. 14. They do not see the salvation that the prophet speaks about. Instead, it appears that God will leave them to perish in exile. God has simply forgotten about them (cf. Isa. 40:27).

53

This cry of anguish is astonishing in light of Yahweh's earlier call to the exiles to be messengers of good news (40:1-11) and the events that permitted those who wished to return to Jerusalem. The actual results, however, had been less than the miracle of renewal for which people hoped. Enemies still remained (v. 17; Ezra 4:1-4).

Formally, the passage consists of an independent hymn of praise (v. 13), followed by the lament of the people (v. 14) and God's reply (vv. 15-18). The reply begins with an analogy between God and a nursing mother (v. 15). It is followed by the assertion that the need for Israel's rebuilding is engraved on God like a tattoo (vv. 16-17). The summons to "lift up your eyes . . . and see," followed by an expression of salvation dawning (v. 18a), is characteristic of this part of Isaiah. Finally, Yahweh swears an oath that Israel will be adorned as a bride (v. 18b).

The lament pattern holds together this section of Isaiah (49:14-26). Verse 14 presents a charge against God; v. 21, a lament by an individual; and v. 24, a lament because enemies hold the speaker captive. We should not think that the promises removed all anxiety and suffering among the people. Psalms of lament were part of worship. The phrasing of v. 14 would have been familiar. The analogy of a nursing mother or a woman aware of the child in the womb indicates how incomprehensible it would be for God to forsake Israel as the lament alleges (v. 15). Nor is the Lord unaware of the fact that Israel needs walls for her defense (v. 16). The enemies cannot tear down the walls of Jerusalem as fast as they can be built (v. 17). The oath in v. 18 introduces another feminine image, the bride adorned with her ornaments. Although Israel now feels abandoned among the nations, she will be the honored center of all just like the bride.

Verse 17 hints at a miraculous transformation. We all know that it takes much longer to build the defensive walls of a city than it does for an invading army to tear them down. This section does not emphasize the process of renewal. It emphasizes the compassion that God feels for the people. This love runs even deeper than that of a mother for her infant. The lesson that Israel should learn from the suffering of exile is not that God has turned away from the people. Rather, God's compassion is demonstrated in this situation because God has not abandoned them. When Israel learns to see God as a mother nursing her infant, Israel will learn to have the same trust in Yahweh that the infant does in the mother.

SECOND LESSON: 1 CORINTHIANS 4:1-13

Although all the apostles are servants of the community, they are not subject to the judgment of that community. Paul returns once again to the problems of boasting and division within the Corinthian church. The heightened tension of this section suggests that the conflict over allegiance to Paul, Apollos, and Cephas (1:12; 3:22) was not merely over choosing a particular side. Charges against Paul himself seem to have been part of the polemic. Paul continues to insist that the weakness of the apostle is a representation of the gospel that he preaches, the crucified Christ.

Formally, this passage can be divided into three sections: (1) an opening argument establishing the court in which the apostle's case is to be judged (vv. 1-5); (2) application to the apostle and his audience, which contains three questions aimed at moving the audience to pass judgment on themselves (vv. 6-7); (3) ironic, ad hominem argument presented in antithetical statements that contrast the Corinthians and the apostle (vv. 8-13). Although the first section establishes an apologetic context for the whole, Paul's defense of his conduct as an apostle is at the same time a condemnation of Corinthian behavior.

The first section begins with an analogy taken from the ancient household. Paul insists that apostles (in this case himself and Apollos, v. 6) are slaves charged with managing the household. Only the owner of the house has the right to judge whether the steward's actions deserve praise or blame. "God's mysteries," which Paul claims are the apostles' charge, must be understood in light of 1 Cor. 2:7 as the preaching of the crucified Christ (vv. 1-2). Verses 3-4 shift from the apostle's task to the question of what tribunal has the right to pronounce judgment. No human being can decide. Although conscience was commonly thought to torment those who violated the norms of good human behavior, Paul does not even grant his own conscience the right to judge his conduct.

Verse 5 suggests a more general principle than the question of whether a church can pass judgment on its apostle/founder. It incorporates two common early Christian views: that God judges what is hidden in the human heart (Matt. 6:4; Heb. 4:12-13; cf. Ps. 139:1, 11-12; Jer. 11:20); and that Jesus will come as judge of all human conduct (1 Thess. 1:10). Based on these convictions, human judgments are ruled out. Paul's own confidence in the integrity of his ministry is not undermined by the conclusion that we can never determine either our own or another's status with God. He anticipates a judgment that will mean praise from God. Some exegetes have suggested that this conclusion also carries a warning and an appeal to those Corinthians who are condemning Paul (and others, cf. 1 Cor. 3:3-4) to repent lest they lose out on the praise they should receive from God.

When Paul turns to apply this analogy with the judgment of stewards by masters to the situation at Corinth, he makes it clear that the Corinthians ought to imitate him. Just as Apollos has assisted Paul in serving the Corinthians, so the Corinthians must learn to see themselves as servants, not masters. The expression, "that you may learn through us (Paul and Apollos)" not to go beyond "what is written" (v. 6) is cryptic. A likely explanation takes "what is written" to refer to Scripture as similar expressions do elsewhere. In that case, Paul is referring to the earlier Scripture passages that warned the Corinthians that God has humbled those who boast in human wisdom and power. Three rhetorical questions charge them with being both presumptuous and ungrateful (v. 7).

The tone sharpens as Paul attacks the Corinthian claims to spiritual perfection. The claim to be one who is rich, a ruler (v. 8), appears in the works of some philosophers, where philosophical wisdom, not material goods, is said to be the true source of nobility and wealth. Paul's characterizations of the Corinthians as wise, strong, and honored (v. 10) invokes the description of their true status earlier (1:26). The apostle, who is the true image of Christ, is the antithesis of this Corinthian picture, a lowly criminal put on display before the whole cosmos—even the angels should be distressed at the sight.

Paul does not limit the contrast to echoes of the degradation of crucifixion in the lowliness of Christ's apostles. He also refers to the hardships that result from his own choice to remain independent of the Corinthians by continuing a slavish way of life, laboring with his hands (vv. 11-12a; cf. 9:14-18; 2 Cor. 12:13-17; 1 Thess. 2:9; 4:11). The apostle has chosen a life that he knows others hold in contempt. Verses 12b-13a point to the response Paul gives to the abuse he suffers as a result of his lowliness in preaching the gospel. Versions of this advice appear elsewhere in the New Testament (Luke 6:28; 23:34; 1 Thess. 5:15; Rom. 12:17). It represents a concrete way in which early Christians practiced Jesus' command to love one's enemies.

Verse 13b sharpens the antithesis between the apostle and the Corinthians as far as possible, likening the apostle to the world's sewer and garbage heap. As we read these words, we instinctively identify with Paul rather than with the Corinthians. Yet most of us are probably more like the Christians at Corinth. We belong to factions in our churches, offices, and communities. We spend lots of energy judging and condemning, and we would not know what to do without our status symbols, whether they are leather jackets or BMWs!

GOSPEL: MATTHEW 6:24-34

For Matt. 5:38-48, see the Seventh Sunday after the Epiphany.

The Corinthians were concerned with religion as a vehicle for honor, human wisdom, and status. As a result, they were unable to appropriate the "foolishness" of God. Matthew 6:24-34 speaks of the material anxieties of life that block a wholehearted devotion to God. As in other readings, analogies are used in the argument to persuade us that our fears and "little faith" (v. 30) are unfounded. Here, the picture of God as creator is drawn in terms of intimate concern for the smallest members of that creation. This image returns in a saying aimed at reassuring disciples when they encounter hostility while preaching the gospel (see Matt. 10:29-31). These images are quite different from pictures of God as creator that emphasize the vastness of creation and the great power of a God who contains all of it (e.g., Job 38:1—41:34). Medieval theologians saw these texts as evidence that God's providence extended to the individual things in the universe. God did not just create the universe with a set of laws and let it run.

Formally, v. 24 is an independent proverb with a brief application to the hearer (cf. Luke 16:13). Verse 25a is the heading to a compendium of sayings on anxiety. The initial conclusion to the group of sayings occurs in the summary (vv. 31-33). Verse 34, which has no counterpart in the parallel Lukan material (Luke 12:22-31), was probably a secondary expansion of the initial collection based on a widespread proverb that the evils of the day are sufficient (v. 34b). Although applicable to the theme, the pessimistic tone of that proverb is quite different from the confidence in God's loving providence shown in the central collection.

Matthew's reader knows that the disciples left family and trades to follow Jesus (4:18-22; 8:19-22). Do these sayings require Christians to do likewise? For the various monastic and mendicant orders that have arisen in Christian history, they have served as the justification for a life of evangelical poverty or radical dependence upon the gifts of others. The evangelist was sensitive to this question as well. The summary suggests that the disciple has a legitimate need for food, clothing, and the like (vv. 31-33). The problem is which shall rule: concern for material security or devotion to the righteousness that characterizes God's rule. There is no virtue in the former—even Gentiles, those without revelation of God, know how to devote themselves to acquiring material possessions. They know how to worry about providing security in a future that is really not under human control. How can we claim to belong to God's rule if we only mirror the standard anxieties of our time?

This section on anxiety also reminds the reader of the Lord's Prayer, which was introduced by exhortations not to be like others. The many words of the Gentiles are unnecessary because God is aware of the needs we bring to prayer (Matt. 6:7-8). The petition for bread can be understood to mean what we need for our sustenance. Consequently, when Matthew adds the epithet "you of little faith" to the conclusion of v. 30, the reader should recognize that the "little faith" implies not trusting the God to whom we pray. We may not accuse God of abandoning us as the Israelites did, but we act as though God were not in the picture.

These verses continue to pose a challenge to Christians. We live in a world dominated by anxieties about material possessions and future security. In our own country, when the economy is in recession everyone holds on a little tighter to whatever he or she has. Even economists can figure out that such behavior is detrimental to the system. We all know people who are so fearful of change that they will not even make changes that would alleviate some of the pain or difficulty in their life. If we really do believe what we pray every day, then we must continue to challenge false anxiety both in ourselves and in our community.

The Transfiguration of Our Lord
Last Sunday after the Epiphany

Lutheran	Roman Catholic	Episcopal	Common Lectionary
Exod. 24:12, 15-18	Dan. 7:9-10, 13-14	Exod. 24:12, 15-18	Exod. 24:12-18
2 Pet. 1:16-19	2 Pet. 1:16-19	Phil. 3:7-14	2 Pet. 1:16-21
Matt. 17:1-9	Matt. 17:1-9	Matt. 17:1-9	Matt. 17:1-9

The Epiphany season closes with the transfiguration. This scene echoes the baptism of Jesus, since God once again declares that Jesus is Son of God. The final manifestation of Jesus' divine sonship comes on the cross. In Matthew's account, the signs of a divine theophany accompany Jesus' death as the Roman soldiers hail Jesus as Son of God (Matt. 27:51-54). Some scholars have suggested that the transfigured appearance of Jesus on a mountain originally belonged to a visionary account of the risen Lord (for the mountain setting see Matt. 28:16). Thus, it is possible to see in the transfiguration an anticipation of Easter as well as the passion.

Early Christian writers, who associated the baptism of Jesus with the incarnation, often saw the transfiguration as proof of Jesus' divine nature. This view omits the salvation history implied in the presence of Moses and Elijah on the mountain. Moses' own encounter with God on Mount Sinai transfigured his face (2 Cor. 3:7-8). Elijah met God on Mount Horeb (1 Kings 19:11-14). Elijah was taken up to heaven in a fiery chariot (2 Kings 1:22). Neither of these earlier heroes of faith can match Jesus' relationship with God.

FIRST LESSON: EXODUS 24:12, 15-18

The impact of this religious vision on human history has been immense. For Jews, it points to the divine gift of the law, which still defines their identity as a people. For Christians, it is a prototype of Jesus' own ministry and vision of God. For Muslims, it is the type of the later revelation of the Koran to the prophet Muhammed. Immediately following this chapter, Exodus contains extensive cultic regulations for worship in the presence of the Lord. Moses' entry into the

Tent of Meeting to intercede for the people was like another return to Sinai. The primary theme of this section of Exodus is Yahweh's presence to Israel. God is present in worship through the cult established around the ark of the covenant. God is also present in the wilderness guiding the people in their wandering.

Formally, this chapter of Exodus consists of a number of disjointed traditions. It has four elements: (1) the people of Israel accept the covenant; (2) the leaders of Israel are prepared and authorized; (3) a continuing presence of God with the people is established; and (4) Moses is singled out as God's special representative. The glory of Yahweh coming to settle on Sinai is described in the poetic language of a theophany or divine appearance. The form of a divine theophany was well established in the ancient world. No one would have thought it necessary to explain this event by assuming, as some modern rationalists do, that Sinai had a volcanic eruption.

The tradition that the Ten Commandments were inscribed on the tablets by God comes from the account in Exod. 34:27-28 where Moses is told to inscribe the ten words on the new tablets that he brings to replace those that had been broken. However, Exod. 24:12 speaks of instruction and commandment, clearly a broader concept of divine revelation. By New Testament times the Pharisees held that God had not only given Moses the written law on Sinai but had also revealed the oral law. This tradition legitimized the practice of expanding the law through interpretation and reinterpretation. No law code can be comprehensive enough to cover the ever-changing variety of human experience. For Israel, Moses' special relationship with God when he alone entered the divine presence on Sinai for forty days makes him the one who can interpret God's will to the people.

Moses' function as leader and judge of the people is grounded in the Sinai experience. Entry into God's presence, especially when that presence is described in the language of glory, also refers to the experience of worship in ancient Israel. Worship takes place in the presence of God. God will be present with the people in the tent sanctuary they are to construct. Here, too, Moses will have special access to the inner part of the sanctuary. When he enters the sanctuary, Moses represents the people before God. Moses will become a mediator between the sinful people and God, pleading with God to withhold the punishment that the nation's sins deserve.

Tradition held that Moses saw the pattern for the sanctuary itself on Sinai (Exod. 25:9; cf. Heb. 8:5). The same pattern was thought to have been used in building the Temple. For the ancient worshiper, entering the Temple was like the experience of the people at Sinai. The Temple area was divided into various courts, just as different persons have different places in relationship to the mountain here. Only the high priest could enter the holiest part of the Temple to carry out the rituals for the Day of Atonement.

Today, most modern Christian churches carry a different message about God's presence. God's presence is not mediated from a sanctuary down through various cultic officials to the worshiper. God's presence is at the focus of a gathered community, mediated to all of them through Jesus' self-offering on the cross.

SECOND LESSON: 2 PETER 1:16-21

Second Peter is our earliest reference to the transfiguration story as it is told in the Gospels. The author introduces the story as evidence for the early Christian belief that Jesus would come again in glory. Evidently, the false teachers against whom the letter speaks had begun to reject this belief (cf. 3:3-7), insisting there was no evidence for such a view. Indeed, the world appeared to them to be continuing as it always had.

Formally, this passage contains two sections: (1) an appeal to the transfiguration as evidence for the truth of apostolic tradition (vv. 16-18); (2) the authority of prophecy as evidence for apostolic teaching (vv. 19-21). Both arguments set a received tradition against the false prophets and private interpretations of Scripture that are troubling the church (vv. 16, 20). The appeal to the transfiguration narrative assumes that the audience knows the account in one of the Gospels. The Gospels, themselves may be included in the Scripture referred to in the second section. Throughout the section, the author speaks in the first person plural, "we." This mode of speech evokes an authority even greater than that of Peter in whose name the letter was written—it claims the authority of all the apostles who witnessed the transfiguration.

Unlike later writers who would see in the transfiguration evidence of Jesus' divinity, and unlike moderns who link the transfiguration with the resurrection and exaltation of Jesus, 2 Peter treats it as evidence for the truth of New Testament claims about the second coming. It is impossible to tell what the sophistic myths told by the opponents were. They might have had an account of Jesus' return to heaven such as that in gnostic circles, which would not allow for any second coming. In such an interpretation, the divine Jesus puts aside the human disguise he wore to enter this world and is reunited with the divine in heaven. Individuals attain salvation by following the path out of this world that Jesus opened up.

The apostles are not only eyewitnesses to Jesus' glory (v. 16); they also hear what God says about Jesus (vv. 17-18). Their testimony is possible because they were on the sacred mountain with Jesus (v. 18). In repeating the transfiguration story, 2 Peter speaks of God giving "honor" and "glory" to Jesus (v. 17). Honor and glory are traditionally attributes of God (cf. 1 Tim. 1:17). The wording of the divine voice combines the voice at the baptism (Matt. 3:17) with the transfiguration account (Matt. 17:5). The author seems to assume that it is because of Jesus' divine status that he will come again. A human being taken up into heaven, as the Roman emperors were said to have been, would not be able to do so.

The argument about prophecy (vv. 19-21) pits sayings inspired by the Holy Spirit against persons who make up their own interpretations. This passage does not mean that 2 Peter thought that Christians should not read the Bible and try to understand its meaning. What they cannot do is engage in idiosyncratic interpretations that deny words the Holy Spirit has inspired. Since these words are in the Scripture, 2 Peter rules out the possibility of others claiming the authority of the Holy Spirit for their teaching.

GOSPEL: MATTHEW 17:1-9

The transfiguration scene follows the first passion prediction (Matt. 16:21-23) and the teaching about discipleship as taking up one's cross (16:24-28). When Peter challenged Jesus' passion prediction, Jesus responded by accusing Peter of thinking the way humans do, not the way God does. The first example of how God thinks comes with the sayings on discipleship. The second example comes indirectly by God's own testimony that Jesus is the beloved Son. Peter leaps to the occasion here too. Acknowledging the extraordinary honor conferred on Jesus, he suggests building shrines or perhaps booths like those used for the Feast of Tabernacles (v. 4). Although it may seem peculiar to us, Peter is attempting to provide a suitable cultic response to this extraordinary event. Verse 9 will indicate why Peter is rebuffed: the transfiguration story cannot be told until after Easter.

Formally, the story of the transfiguration is similar to the account of the baptism: (1) setting (vv. 1-2); (2) "suddenly" (v. 3a) followed by the vision (v. 3); (3) "suddenly" (v. 5a) followed by the divine word (v. 5). Matthew has drawn on the Markan version (Mark 9:5-8). Since the episode is a revelation scene, some gesture of fear is expected (v. 6). As he does elsewhere, Matthew avoids the Markan suggestion that the disciples were terrified (Mark 9:6). He has them prostrate themselves in awe, a gesture of worship.

Peter's proposal (v. 4) intrudes on the structure derived from the baptism scene. It anticipates the dialogue between Jesus and the disciples about Elijah on the way down from the mountain (vv. 9-13). Peter's comment in v. 4 also transforms the divine voice from its function as a revelation formula identifying Jesus to a rebuke of the apostle. The command, "listen to him!" (v. 5) underlines the possibility that the disciples will not be obedient to Jesus' word. Matthew lessens the negative portrayal of the disciples implicit in this divine warning by situating the disciples' awed reaction after the voice has spoken. Normally, it would come with the appearance of the divine presence in the bright cloud (v. 3; cf. Matt. 28:17). Traditionally, a heavenly revealer would reassure the troubled visionary (cf. Rev. 1:17-18). Here, Matthew has added that detail to his source (v. 7). Instead of serving as the prelude to the divine revelation, Jesus' reassurance terminates the vision. Where Mark had the episode leave the disciples perplexed and in fear, Matthew has the dialogue end with their understanding that John the Baptist was the coming Elijah.

Peter and the sons of Zebedee, James and John, were the first disciples called to follow Jesus (Matt. 4:18-22). Their willingness to leave family and occupation in order to answer the call made them examples for later followers of Jesus. In this episode, they receive a privileged revelation about Jesus' heavenly status. Matthew has added, "his face shone like the sun," to Mark's glistening white garments (Mark 9:3; Matt. 17:2). The shining face recalls the transfiguration of Moses' face (Exod. 34:29-35). It reappears in the vision of the risen Jesus in glory that opens Revelation (Rev. 1:16). Despite Peter's false step in proposing that booths be built for Jesus, Elijah, and Moses, the disciples do come to understand who Jesus is. By the end of the concluding dialogue, they also recognize the Baptist as the Elijah figure who was to precede the Messiah. Where the Markan picture of the disciples is in ambiguous terms, Matthew redraws the story to indicate that the disciples' response to Jesus was always exemplary for other Christians.

The divine voice that commands obedience to Jesus' word points toward the conclusion of the Gospel. The risen Jesus instructs the disciples to teach the nations to keep his word (28:20). This command is possible because Jesus has been endowed with "all authority in heaven and on earth" (28:18). Throughout the Gospel, Jesus' word and his position as God's chosen one belong together. Jesus can command the obedience of all peoples because of his unique relationship to God. The universality of Jesus' mission may be implicit in the appearance of Moses and Elijah. Jesus is clearly intended to be greater than Israel's lawgiver and one of her greatest prophetic figures, both of whom had had visions of God.

Jesus is not simply a Jewish messiah. Already in this vision we have a hint of something greater. But the revelation of that truth cannot be given publicly until after the death and resurrection of Jesus (v. 9). However, the understanding and obedience that the disciples demonstrate are already examples for those who would come after them. Thus, the transfiguration also reminds us that we do not follow Jesus because he was a wise person or even one who gave God's law to a nation, as Moses had done. Jesus does not stand in the line of prophetic figures like Elijah. Jesus' word is more than all these, since it is the word of God's beloved Son.